Restoring
Antique
Furniture

Restoring
Antique
Furniture

Edwin Johnson

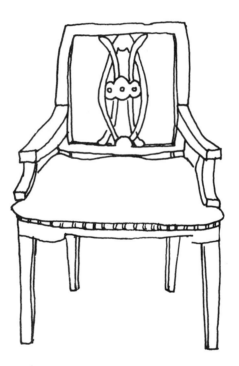

Sterling Publishing Co., Inc. New York

Drawings by Pamela J. Johnson.

Photographs by Jim Kuba.

Photographs on pages 63, 117, 120, 121 and 122 courtesy of
Fine Hardwoods/American Walnut Association.

Library of Congress Cataloging in Publication Data

Johnson, Edwin.
   Restoring antique furniture.

   (Home craftsman series)
   Includes index.
   1. Furniture—Repairing. 2. Furniture finishing.
3. Upholstery. I. Title. II. Series.
TT199.J627   1981   749'.1'0288   81-50987
ISBN 0-8069-5430-2   AACR2
ISBN 0-8069-5431-0 (lib. bdg.)
ISBN 0-8069-8998-X (pbk.)

Copyright © 1982 by Sterling Publishing Co., Inc.
Two Park Avenue, New York, N.Y. 10016
Distributed in Australia by Oak Tree Press Co., Ltd.
P.O.Box J34, Brickfield Hill, Sydney 2000, N.S.W.
Distributed in the United Kingdom by Blandford Press
Link House, West Street, Poole, Dorset BH15 1LL, England
Distributed in Canada by Oak Tree Press Ltd.
℅ Canadian Manda Group, 215 Lakeshore Boulevard East
Toronto, Ontario M5A 3W9
Manufactured in the United States of America

Contents

1   Restoring Antique Furniture

You bought (or borrowed) this book because you want to strip and refinish that old rocker or that peeling armoire or some other old antique piece that has been taking up space in the basement all these years—or that you bought for a song. Good for you! Join the many thousands who are absorbed in a joyful and valuable avocation. I call them the weekend strippers and evening refinishers.

These antique restorers dash home from shop, office or campus, perhaps gulping a hamburger on the way, change into their grubbiest jeans and begin another four-hour stint of sanding and scraping and staining furniture that is old, dusty and often in pathetic disrepair. All over the country, otherwise normal people are doing without their usual TV fare or their tennis—all because they want attractive antiques. And I think that's wonderful!

Can You Learn from a Book?

The answer is yes; and I am the living proof. It has been almost ten years since I began restoring antique furniture. It started with my haunting garage sales with my wife in Oak Park, Illinois. When we amassed a basementful of Victorian pieces in poor condition, a friend gave me a book on restoring furniture. What I learned from the book, combined with my own expertise as a wood sculptor, enabled me to refinish all our collection and sell most of it to a local antiques dealer. I was in business.

Word got out, and I began doing restorations for other dealers and customers. I knew I had become established when, in the fall of 1977, I was asked to restore the original Frank Lloyd Wright family dining furniture that was to be housed in the restored dining room of his first home and studio in Oak Park, Illinois.

Since then, the experience I have gained and the authorities from whom I have learned so much, made me confident that I could write this book to help you get started.

There are, without doubt, many methods for achieving a given restoration result. Some techniques and materials are quite controversial; for example, what type of glue to use or whether to use tung oil. In this book I focus on the easiest and most effective methods—some which I have developed and some which I have borrowed. But in every case, these are techniques which have worked well for me, whether I've used them in the simplest of refinishing jobs or the most challenging and ornery restorations.

Nonantique Restorers Are Also Welcome

You don't have to want to restore only antique pieces to read my book and get a lot from it. Fixing up any old furniture will suffice. Recently, I restored a 20-year-old maple table that was slightly scratched and that had a few water rings on the top. My customer wanted the table to better match a grouping of Golden Oak antiques (p. 148) in which she was going to place it. The techniques in this book were applied to that job, and success was the outcome.

Why Restore Antique Furniture?

Obviously, antique furniture is worth preserving, if for no other reason than for its market value. A good deal of the furniture that is simply old right now also is worth preserving because it will be the antique of tomorrow.

The principal reason why antiques command such high prices has to do with the law of supply and demand. The supply of antiques is limited due to our small population in olden times, while the demand today is huge.

The economic side of furniture restoration is important in another respect. Not only do antiques increase in value with the passing years, but many still can be acquired at prices below those of new pieces. A customer asked me to restore a huge, birch, built-in butler's pantry. It was 12 ft. (3.6 m) long and 8 ft. (2.4 m) high, and had three large, double-glass-door upper cabinets with beadboard backs, a solid birch countertop, an 18-in. (45.7-cm)-high solid birch splashboard, and a lower cabinet housing six deep drawers.

Among the antiques my wife and I collected are some noteworthy bargains, too: Our Biedermeier chest (c. 1840), a small, three-drawer Victorian chest in cherrywood, and a Golden Oak plant table. Granted that these and others were acquired in very sorry condition—nevertheless, the economics still favor us when you consider their present worth.

There are other compelling reasons for restoring antiques. Perhaps you have an ugly, painted oak table. Perhaps the piece is not useful in its present condition: It has a broken leg, a warped top, an unhinged drop leaf or an uncaned chair bottom. You want to restore and preserve the table because it has sentimental value for you. It is rumored to be your great-great-grandmother's, but you can't identify it because of all the dirt and varnish covering it. Then, too, many of us would like to pass on to our children important heirlooms, just as some of our parents did for us.

Finally, the quality of many old and antique pieces is higher than that found in much of the furniture made today. Our early Pennsylvania cupboard is made from 1-in. (2.5-cm)-thick cherry wood. Of course, it is as heavy as a small piano, but the quality is there. Once you realize that most modern furniture veneers are very thin—and that under these are composite boards of some sort—can there be any doubt as to the advantages of buying old and antique pieces and fixing them yourself?

Empire chest (1835). It is a German Biedermeier made of pine carcass and topped with pearwood veneer and maple columns, plinths and trim. This chest is small for chests of this period; hardware is old but not original. Has been refinished natural.

What Is Restoration?

Restoration is the process of returning a piece of furniture to its original form, quality and function. This process entails repair, correction of finish deficiencies and replacement of missing parts.

From this process a sort of "restorer's philosophy" emerges. It is, quite simply, that you should be as faithful to the original as possible. This means that you should identify the original style and period of the item (even if it means going to the books and/or museums to research it). See Chapter 8 for information on characteristics of various period pieces.

Take, for example, one of my most important jobs—the restoration of the original Frank Lloyd Wright dining room suite.

The valuable six side chairs were originally Victorian with Jacobean barley-twist spindles in their backs, and in typical Wright style, were high-backed and narrow. Wright had them remodelled to reflect his developing Prairie School period motifs, and they received a coat or two of a dark, oak varnish stain to duplicate the fumed oak color of Mission furniture.

Restoration included repair, as well as refinishing and re-upholstering. While the Mission-style chair-back spindles were left, the color was returned to that of golden oak, a faithful duplication of the original.

Here the author is shown refinishing an original Frank Lloyd Wright chair from the Frank Lloyd Wright Home and Studio Foundation in Oak Park, Illinois.

Antiques Needing Repair

Almost every antique chair seems to need some sort of repair. This is because chairs, of all furniture items, take the worst beating. Perhaps there is a loose or missing stretcher, a loose leg, a broken bottom spindle or rocker.

Some well-meaning but inexpert former owners often tried to rectify these problems by applying what I call the "carpenter's repair." The philosophy in these cases was: If one nail was good, ten were ten times as good. Glue was rarely used, and when it was, two no-no's were employed: The old glue was not removed, and the repair was not clamped. Another common error was to strip off the old finish, and *then* to make the repair. Since glue makes wood unreceptive to good refinishing, the result was often spotty and discolored.

So, another reason many of us want to get involved in restoration is that we want to correctly repair our precious antiques. Such activity not only preserves the item, but returns it to usefulness. After all, what good is a rocker if you can't rock in it, or a chest of drawers if it has no drawer bottoms?

Restoration Out of Sheer Necessity

Finally we come to these extreme situations: Every time you pull up a chair to your rolltop desk you worry that it will come crashing down; you avoid watering your plant because you're sure the lopsided stand will soon tip over; you sit gingerly on those rickety, pressed-back chairs or serious injury may result. These are not *usual* repair situations; they are *crises* to be resolved immediately!

When veneer is lifting or paint is peeling off a child's high chair and could easily be eaten, that's a crisis! And this book can help you solve these crises. You'll learn how to make all sorts of repairs and how to remove deteriorating finishes—simply, easily, successfully.

Getting Ready to Restore

Since nothing succeeds like success, I suggest that you undertake a small job first—a wooden recipe box or a mirror frame, perhaps. Put off the really rough jobs until you've acquired a little skill, more confidence, or both.

Know what to expect from your efforts. If you're not sure, browse through antique shows, museums with fine furniture exhibits, antiques shops and the homes of friends where restored furniture can be seen—or better yet, in use!

Still other ways to acquire knowledge, and with it more confidence, are to work on a local restoration project—perhaps at the home of one of your community's famous residents—or to help a friend with his or her recent antique acquisition.

Eclectic dining room, above: Steuben light fixture with gold auren shades (c. 1905); walnut Eastlake mirror frame (c. 1880); maple server bought as unfinished furniture (c. 1970); elmwood side chairs (c. 1910); Golden Oak dining table (c. 1900); and hand-painted Art Deco candlestick holders (c. 1927). A closer view of the Golden Oak dining table and elmwood side chairs is shown on the following page.

Be Organized

You've just got to be organized to bring off a good job. A sane approach is to divide up the job into workable units. Decide how much time you have and attempt only what you can complete in that time period. Take, for example, restoring a round oak table with center pedestal, six chairs and three table boards. If you plan to strip them all in the evenings after supper, do the table boards first and get a "feel" for the finish. Then strip one chair a night; that should take from two to five hours, depending on the finish and the complexity. Strip the table last. Since it's deceptively easy, it should take one evening. The total? Eight evenings of work so far.

For the refinishing, I would figure two nights to sand and clean up the residue. Then take a Saturday to stain, so you can complete all pieces in an eight-hour day. Let it all stand until the next weekend, then take another Saturday and seal everything. This time, it won't take all day—at least, it shouldn't!

All that remains at this point is the finish coat, and you can plan on finishing a piece an evening. How long for the entire job? About a month.

Restoration Guidelines

Keep in mind several restoration guidelines as you work on antique furniture. They are:

1. All your restoration work should be capable of being reversed. That is, finishes should be easily removable at a future date. So don't put a laminated plastic top on your round oak table with mastic and nails; don't nail where only glue is needed to hold, and don't sink dowels in such a way as to prohibit disassembly later.

2. Your work should be faithful to the original style and design, the original color and even the original finish of the piece. However, it was very popular for a while to cut down small, oval, Empire period occasional tables for use as coffee tables and to refinish Victorian walnut pieces in a light shade instead of its natural dark color. As to finish, shellac was commonly used; however, since it is an impractical coating compared with modern finishes, it is permissible to depart from faithfulness to the original in this case.

3. Finally, think *repair*, not *replace*. It's a great temptation to replace a chair stretcher or seat with a new one, particularly when there's evidence of scratches, splits and breaks. You decide repair is not worth the time and effort. Well, it is!

Sources of Antiques

Antique furniture can still be found in attics, basements and barns, though they may be well disguised with ten coats of paint or 30 years of dust and dirt. The flea market has become an important antique source in some areas where both finished and rough pieces are available, sometimes at very low prices. Garage sales are still a source, and depending on where you live and how many you can go to on a Saturday morning, you will probably find something useful.

Antique dealers, however, are a much more reliable and constant source of antiques. If you are seriously looking for a given item and are willing to pay more, the dealer is just the right person to approach. All dealers will negotiate, although the extent varies as to the amount and the time period of the piece.

At a major antique show, you will find a very convenient assemblage of antiques, often from various parts of the country. You can also study generally well-restored pieces or some that are in excellent original condition, and learn standards for your efforts. Such a show makes possible comparison between various dealers in little time. The drawback is that you will pay for the quality you buy; there are no bargains, but I think there is good value.

Buyer's Kit

When shopping for an antique, carry a buyer's kit. It should contain a tape measure, a magnifying glass, magnet and a flashlight. The magnifying glass is useful when searching for markings, and the magnet tells you when something is not solid brass. Flashlights are helpful when looking inside cabinets, under tables, and at the backs of case goods. To help in reducing impulse-buying, carry a list of what you wish to buy and stick to it.

What to Look for

Basically, one should look for signs of genuineness in the item, and I don't mean necessarily a date on the back of a chest or the bottom of a chair. Use construction details outlined in Chapter 8 as a supplement to the identifiable style.

It is helpful to examine the back of a piece of furniture. Pieces of the late nineteenth century have heavier backboards than subsequent pieces, and they run vertically. Backs also tell whether a "marriage" has taken place. Consider a two-piece country cupboard. Do the backs match in board direction, board width and board appearance? If so, they have been together since their beginning. If not, they are a marriage. You can still buy such a piece, but it's worth less. And if the finish is either poor or painted over, you have no indication of the success of your restoration if the woods are really different. Finally, backs generally still have visible saw marks. It is helpful for dating purposes to know that circular saw marks appear on furniture made after 1850.

Dovetailing is another thing to look at. In chests and cupboards, it can be seen in the drawer sides; in trunks, at the corners. Machine-cut dovetailing is usually perfect, whereas the hand-cut variety usually shows saw cuts beyond those necessary for joining the piece. Most hand-cut dovetailing was done before the Civil War.

Remember also the rule of dovetailing: the fewer the number, the older the antique piece. Only two dovetail joints appear in drawers made between 1725 and 1800, and only three are present in early Empire pieces. Early dovetails are much narrower than later ones.

Hand-cut drawer lock cavities also show saw marks beyond the actual cavity. Look at drawer bottoms. Older pieces have bevelled drawer bottoms, and the oldest have hand-planed ones. Look at panelled doors on cupboards: The older ones show evidence of hand-planing.

Hinges should also be examined. H-shaped hand-forged ones are found in original American Colonial pieces, and long, thin hinges are older than shorter, wider ones. The oldest screws in the hinges are very thin-slotted, so thin in fact, that a modern screwdriver cannot unscrew them. If you can get the screw out, note the threads; uneven threads indicate they were hand-cut and are very old.

Nails, too, tell their tale. Square nails are older than round ones; still older ones are uneven in appearance, indicating that they are hand-wrought. Run your magnet over "brass" hinges and other such hardware; if the magnet clings, the hardware is iron or steel, has been plated, and is not old.

Wood species also aid in determining the age of a piece. Board dimensions are another age determinant. One-in. (2.5-cm-) thick boards are often found in Country and Primitive furniture that is truly old. Wider boards, too, were common in earlier times. Many early chests were called six-board chests because that's all it took to make them!

Check for "roundness." If a leg is perfectly round, it is not old, because wood shrinks disproportionately with age.

While it is possible to fake antiques, it is not worth the time nor the trouble in the great majority of instances. So while faking is not widespread, old (but not original) copies do exist. Some were produced by firms during the United States Centennial Celebration in 1876, and some were made in high-school wood shops. Still other copies were made by rural dwellers during the long winters. So while the piece *is* old and *is* handmade, it is not necessarily a valuable antique.

2 *Antique Furniture Repairs Made Easy*

The old proverb, "A stitch in time saves you nine" most certainly can be applied to repairing furniture. Defects get worse, not better, with time, and the worse they get, the more "stitches" will be needed. In addition, repair is much easier to do before stripping and refinishing.

You may have been hoping to put off the repairs and get to the "fun" part immediately. After all, the new finish is what shows. You may not see any need for repairing your particular piece—that is, you've refinished a wobbly chair that then falls apart! Then, too, repair work can be tedious and frustrating, especially if you're a beginner, so you put it off . . . and off.

Well, I can help you to identify defects and what you have to do to correct them. You *can* learn how to make repairs quickly and easily.

How to Tell if Repairs Are Needed

A general principle is that nearly *all* antiques need some degree of repair. So, the first step is to look for structural problems.

THE KNEE TEST. Set a chair on the floor, put your knee on the seat, grasp the back and push it and pull it back and forth. If front legs, back uprights, rear legs —or all three—are becoming loose, they will show up in this test.

Now try to pull the back top rail loose from its uprights; turn the chair over, set it on its back on the floor, and try to pull the legs apart. Take a hammer and strike the underside of the seat, holding the chair by a leg in midair, to test if the legs are still glued into the seat. See if the stretchers turn. Examine the underside of the seat for splits if it is solid, or the seat rails if it is caned or upholstered. Any separation or previous glueing indicates the presence of a problem.

THE ROCKING TEST. Attempt to rock chests of drawers and tables. Remove drawers, set them on their side and try to rock them, too. Try to move the table while it's standing on its legs. If possible, turn the table over on its top and try to move each leg or the center pedestal. Anything that moves is loose and needs to be repaired.

THE TAPPING TEST. With your finger, tap side panels in chests and cabinets as well as panels on doors. A hollow sound or rattling indicates looseness. Tapping also indicates whether or not veneer is loose.

17

(Above) A Chippendale chair, badly in need of repair, is shown in the author's shop; it is also in need of refinishing and reupholstering.

(Opposite) The author is conducting the knee test. The back legs and back uprights are coming loose from the side rails.

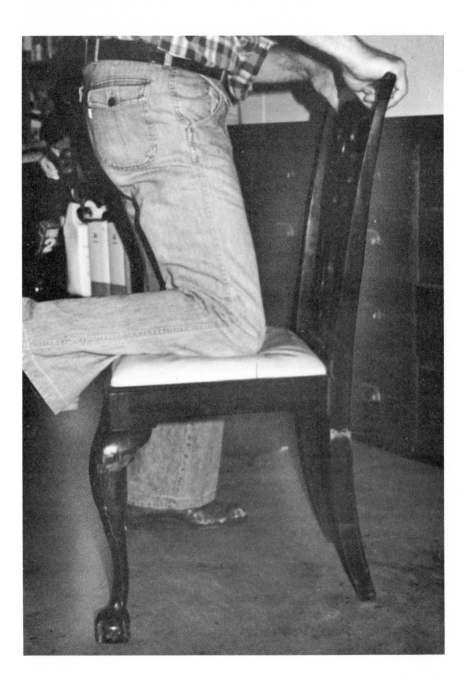

THE LIFTING TEST. The best test for any antique piece with a top is to lift it. Simply lift the piece and if the top is loose, you'll know it.

A word of caution is in order here. Of course, I'm not suggesting that you *look* for trouble. If your particular antique seems to be in fine condition, seems sturdy, and successfully passes the tests, leave it be.

The Repair Process

In any technical procedure you must use the correct tools, materials and techniques. A specific listing of what you'll need to own and to know follows.

TOOLS. Simple hand tools are used for furniture repair and are probably already in your toolbox. They are a wood saw, coping saw, wooden mallet, crowbar, several putty knives, wire cutters and a pair of pliers.

Your toolbox may not contain clamps; if not, buy a few. Clamps come in two basic configurations—C-clamps and pipe clamps. C-clamps can be either of wooden or metal construction; wooden clamps are designed for furniture work but are heavy and too expensive for occasional repairs. Metal C-clamps are more practical and cost at least half of their wooden counterpart.

Pipe clamps are generally purchased without the pipe; the two ends come in a package and fit any ¾-in. (19-mm) pipe. Buy the pipe the length you need and have one end threaded; I suggest you buy several 2-foot (.6-m) lengths and several 3-foot (.9-m) lengths to begin with. If you intend to do very limited repairs, you may only need one pair of threaded rods with nuts and washers holding a common piece of wood between them at each end. The resulting long "O" shape will do a lot of holding for a low price, but it is inconvenient to use. The really bargain-basement holding device is a rope "tourniquet." A couple of pairs of pipe clamps, though, is your best investment.

GLUE. Always, always, use glue *unless* another fastener is specifically called for in the original design, as screws are in Mission furniture. It is virtually the only material you will need.

Metal is undesirable as a bonding agent because it wears wood at joined points, especially where resistance to movement is important. Further, metal can split wood. Finally, metal in the form of nails and screws comes loose much sooner than properly glued joints. So avoid not only nails and screws, but metal braces and brackets as well.

There are several kinds of glues available. My choice has always been a water-soluble synthetic adhesive.

The other popular glue is what I call "traditional" because it is touted by some of the old professional craftsmen. It is a hot glue made by heating a cake of powder glue and applying it while hot. Although a "glue controversy" is currently raging, I maintain that the old, hot glue is overrated. My opinion is based on my constantly repeated experience of repairing work in which that material was the only holding power, and it failed to hold.

A sort of compromise adhesive material, which combines good holding power and ease of application, is the hot glue gun. Its advantage is that it glues items that can't be clamped or that are unnecessary to clamp. You simply squirt in the glue, hold the assembly until it sets—which is rapid—and presto, it's repaired!

THE GLUEING PROCESS. There are six steps to the glueing process:

1. Pull or knock the piece or assembly apart.

2. Clean off all old, dried glue.

3. Apply glue to a limited number of dowels, tenons and surfaces.

4. Put together subassemblies, such as backs, sides, drawers. Then clamp.

5. Assemble subassemblies, clamp and leave to set on a level surface.

6. Clean off excess glue.

• *Step One.* Extremely loose joints can be pulled apart by hand. This is really the safest method of disassembly as it is very easy to damage antique furniture at this point. Care is the byword because old wood is often very dry and brittle.

Force *is* necessary. To assist your muscles, I recommend various crowbars, a wooden mallet and a hammer. When using these and other tools, protect your piece from damaging tool marks. Wrap a heavy rag around a turned element when striking it with a wooden mallet or hammer and place a scrap of wood (caul) on a flat surface when striking it. Panel frames can be separated by placing the end of a 1 × 2 × 3-in. (2.5 × 5.1 × 7.6-cm) scrap against the inside edge and striking the other end of the scrap with a hammer.

Crowbars should pry from the reverse or underneath side wherever possible to reduce tool damage. Take, for example, the separation from its base of a large oak tabletop constructed of seven 8-in. (20-cm) boards, each held to the other with eight dowels. I would flip the top over on its trestle and begin separating the boards at one end with a small, thin crowbar, working my way along and between two joined boards at a time. As the separation grows wider, I would insert the larger crowbar, making sure that it came in contact only with the underneath side of the joining seam. A crowbar extending through the seam could nick the top surface edge, and such a defect would remain.

Protect all exterior wood surfaces that will later show. Use less, rather than more, muscle, and look for hidden nails. Old repairs, usually by handymen, often entailed small finishing nails that may not now be visible. Chair stretchers, spindles, top rails and splats are frequently held in this manner. If the component is loose and yet won't separate, you know a nail is there somewhere. Once you've found it, try to saw it or cut it somehow. You may be able to pull it through with pliers. If those attempts are unsuccessful, about the only thing left is to dig it out with a pair of fine-point cutting pliers. A hole results, often a large one, which you patch after the sealing step in refinishing.

It is a good idea to record how the piece is constructed, consecutively number parts, or otherwise remember how it's put together. Naturally, do this before you take it all apart. Never count on similar pieces, such as Windsor chair spindles, going back in any order. Time does strange things to old furniture, so you'd best number the parts or attach masking tape to individual parts and number them.

• *Step Two.* As new glue will *never* stick to old, remove all old glue. To get it off flat surfaces, use a half-round rasp, file or coarse sandpaper. For curved surfaces such as stretcher ends, I use a riffler—a small, curved rasp. To clean glue out of dowel holes, match a drill bit to the exact size of the hole and carefully drill out old glue. Mortise joints require more time and care: Use a sharp chisel and the end of a rasp.

When it is impossible to get the old glue out, use new dowels and dowel holes, and new tenon-and-mortise joints. If the abundance of glue is clearly synthetic, try soaking it off since it is water soluble.

• *Step Three.* When applying glue, you don't put too much on too many parts in advance because the glue will dry up. On the other hand, efficient work demands that you do some advance glueing. For example, a Windsor chair-back assembly consists of the seat, a number of spindles and a curved top rail. To glue this together, place glue in each spindle hole in the chair seat, allow small drops to run down the side of the hole, and lightly glue the bottom end of each spindle, wiping off the excess. Then place the spindles in their respective holes, and put drops of glue in the top-rail spindle holes while the rail is upside down so the glue can run in those holes. I then apply glue on the tops of all spindles, and tap the rail into place. Note that *all* joined areas are glued to assure a good job, and excess glue is wiped off before it sets.

• *Step Four.* The foregoing example of glueing a Windsor chair is also an illustration of what I call a subassembly. Others are a drawer, four chair legs and stretchers, a chest backboard, and a glued-up tabletop. I prefer to put a subassembly together first. At times I can proceed and complete the assembly, say, the entire chair. Other times, particularly with large pieces, I prefer to clamp subassemblies and allow them to set. I then put them together and clamp the

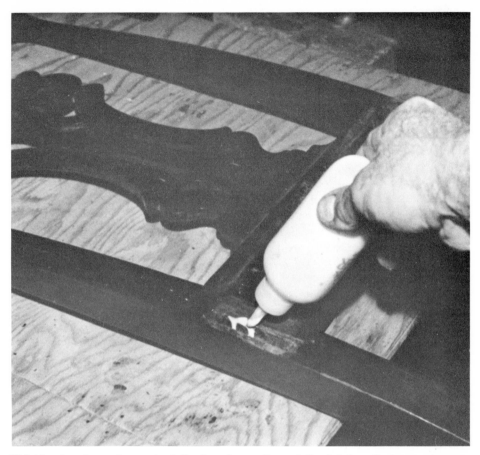

Old glue has been dug out of the female portion of the joint so that new glue can then be applied.

entire piece. There is no set rule: What you do is governed by the size of the piece. Be certain, however, that everything in the subassembly is square and will properly go into the whole piece. For example, drawers must be checked for squareness, and the chest carcass should not be clamped so tightly that the drawers will not fit in their openings!

• *Step Five.* In this step you put together all the different glueing stages. I'll illustrate this step with a solid oak Frank Lloyd Wright table that's 4 × 8 ft. (1.2 × 2.4 cm). The top typically has a rectangular skirt attached to the top edge to give it a mass it doesn't naturally possess. Together with the seven boards, they make up the top subassembly. The square hollow legs in each corner are paired and connected by crosspieces, and each of these makes up two more subassemblies.

Final assembly consists of glueing and clamping the two pairs of legs together with the long top rails and a solid shelf at the bottom. Be sure the piece is sitting on a level surface, that chair backs are square with seats, and that pieces do not lean. A vexing problem with chairs is that after you have everything fully assembled and clamped, one leg may seem longer than the others. Solution: Place the chair feet of the "longer" diagonal line on small pieces of a one-by-two on the floor and put pressure on the chair corners that are not on these wood pieces. Set the chair square on the floor to see if it does not rock. If it still does not sit square, try straightening it again. This generally works, but if it doesn't, loosen one set of clamps a little since the clamps may be on too tight.

Using clamps is the only way to repair. The hydrostatic pressure built up in dowel-and-mortise holes by the wet glue forces a joint slightly apart unless it's held by a clamp. That small separation often enlarges with use of the furniture over time, and it will then be necessary to repair again! Proper use of clamps avoids this problem.

• *Step Six.* Clean off all excess glue before it sets by simply taking a rag with warm water and quickly mopping it up.

Major Repair Problems

Armed with the rules and principles of good antique furniture repair, let's now turn to specific repair problems and my recommendations on how to solve them.

Breaks

While all kinds of furniture pieces and components break, I've found the most common are chair legs and backs. Running a close second is the table leg, followed by drawers in chests and bureaus.

(Opposite) The seat and back assembly are being held together by pipe clamps. Note that thick pads of newspaper protect the chair from any scratching the metal clamps may cause, as well as excessive pressure. The wooden braces holding the side rails to the back rail will be glued and screwed into place after making certain that all old glue has been removed.

In the case of a chair leg and a related component, the spindle, remove it from the furniture piece, if possible. Squirt plenty of synthetic glue on both ends of the break and pull the element together with a pipe clamp. If the break is at all diagonal, place a small C-clamp across it, providing horizontal pressure as well. Wipe excess glue with a wet rag and be sure to allow at least 24 hours for the glue to set properly.

Broken dowels, spindles and chair legs where some wood remains in the receiving hole can be handled by getting the wood out of the hole. I do this by making the break flush with the dowel-hole rim and mark its center with a scratch awl or ice pick. Then, using a drill bit the diameter of the hole, I drill out the remaining wood, taking care to follow the angle of the hole. If the break is deep inside the dowel hole, I apply glue to both ends of the break, reinsert the broken spindle or other part, and clamp it up.

When breaks require that material be drilled out of a hole, the stretcher or other component has been shortened. To bring it to its proper length, you can do one of several things. A new piece can be made, an extension piece can be joined by a tenon-and-mortise joint, or one can refill the dowel hole with the correct diameter dowel and drill out the end of the broken stretcher and the filled dowel hole for a smaller diameter dowel. For example, a ⅜-in. (9.5-mm) dowel could hold a ¾-in. (19-mm) stretcher. Be sure, however, not to let the repair dowel show!

Because of the heavy stress placed on rocking chairs, their breaks should be repaired by using either a dowel to hold the two pieces of the broken rocker together, or by mortising a piece of wood into the bottoms of the broken pieces to hold them together. Glue and clamp the mortised piece in place.

Splits

Generally, splits should not be ignored, even if they don't show. For example, the part of the drawer side on which it slides is often split under where it is joined by the drawer bottom, or a board in the backboard is split at the bottom where it extends below the chest or cabinet bottoms. Such splits can expand and cause both structural weaknesses and eventually aesthetic ugliness as well if they are not repaired in time.

Splits take the form of split chair bottoms, cabinet and wardrobe door panels, all sorts of side panels in carcasses, solid members, and glued members of pieces such as melodion desk legs. In general, the approach to correcting splits is to squirt as much glue as possible into the split and properly clamp it until the glue sets. Some splits defy the entrance of glue, however. In that case, widen the split, using a knife, and then get the glue in. Be careful not to make either a tool mark or a clamp mark, and be careful to avoid making a split a break. Breaks necessitate exact placing of the broken parts to make the job look good.

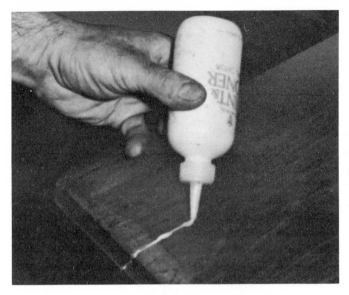

Glue is being put into one of the two wide splits. The splits are wide enough to enable the glue to seep downward.

To make sure that there is enough glue in the split, apply slight pressure with a finger.

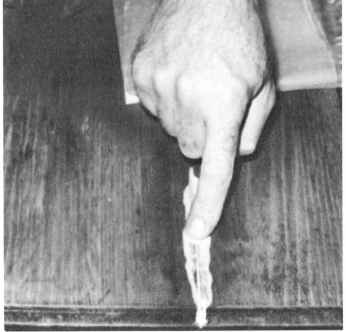

27

Clamping the split is accomplished by using a longer clamp to pull the split together, and using a small C-clamp or two to insure a matching of surfaces of the divergent parts. Here's how it's done: Place a piece of waxed paper on the top and under the bottom of the split panel and a short ¾-in. (19-mm) piece of caul on the waxed paper pieces across the split (use two or more cauls if the split is a long one). Loosely clamp the cauls to level the surface sides of the split and pull the split together by placing a long C-clamp or a pipe clamp at the widest part of the split and tighten it. Now tighten the C-clamps and wipe away any glue that has been pushed out of the panel split.

Pieces of waxed paper are placed over the repairs to prevent the wood cauls from sticking to the furniture piece.

Long wood cauls are placed over the waxed paper because the top of the table is warped.

You can also correct previous component split repairs where old glue and plaster or plastic wood filler were used in a futile attempt to cover up the splits. Clean out all of the old glue or filler or both to insure a successful repair. If this is impossible, you can patch or fill.

It certainly helps to remove the split component from the furniture carcass, legs or rails to repair it. This is especially true of panels, be they a part of the door, the carcass side or the drawer bottom. Generally, this can be accomplished by removing one side of the panel frame first. You can then slide the panel out. If the frame won't budge, glue the split in the panel by nailing cauls to either side of the split on the inside of the panel, taking care not to nail through to the outside. Put glue in the split and clamp the cauls together, pulling the split parts with it.

Solid members such as a Boston rocker leg or a chair arm which have been split can, of course, be corrected by the glue-and-clamp method. Some large members like the cyma curved leg and foot projections of extension tables are made of a number of pieces of wood that have been glued together. Dampness often causes some of these wood laminates to separate. Here, you should try to get out some of the old glue. Take a folded piece of sandpaper, insert it in the split and work it around. Then insert lots of glue, clamp and let set.

The test of your skill in repairing splits is the tabletop. Such splits differ from splits on panels and other components in that they are larger, and thicker, *and* they show. Tops of occasional tables, plant stands and the like are generally made from one piece of wood. Often the split accompanies warping, which should be corrected first. Remove the top if possible so that skirts do not impede wood movement. Treat the top like a panel; glue, making sure you get plenty all the way through the split, and C-clamp over cauls and waxed paper to ensure a level job. Clamp across, starting at the widest end of the split. For larger tops and splits, you may need two or more pipe clamps. After tightening the C-clamps, wipe up excess glue.

Despite all this you may still get slightly different levels or a slight gap after the repair has set due to the different parts of the split going their own way after the split occurred. Sometimes splits exist for years under very adverse environmental conditions, the result being that repair is impossible. It is best not to count on either sanding or filling to correct any level or gap deficiencies. Sanding here will lighten the surface adjacent to the split, causing it to refinish lighter. Sanding the entire surface will make it lighter than the rest of the piece, giving you refinishing problems. Filling tabletop cracks is a job for an expert because anything less than perfection usually looks worse than the split.

The table has been clamped and will be placed in a dry place for two days so that the glue can dry properly.

When they do split, solid wood tabletops generally split along the joining edges of the component boards that make up this top. Such boards are joined either with glue or with glued dowels. Glued joints can either be a tongue-and-groove arrangement or flat surfaces that are only joined with glue. The latter is obviously the trickiest to repair because a level surface should be the outcome. Be sure to clamp at right angles to the split as well as across it.

In the case of tongue-and-groove joints, try to get all of the old glue out of the separation. With dowel joinings, it is possible that the dowel may be loose in *both* its holes; therefore, try to completely separate the split and, using pliers, test the dowel in the hole for looseness. Clean glue off all exposed dowels and out of all dowel holes, reglue, clamp, wipe off excess glue, and let set.

Looseness and loose pieces

To correct loose door panels in cabinets, cupboards and wardrobes, remove the door and try to disassemble the frame around the panel, removing at least one side of the frame. Apply glue to both the panel edge going into the frame and into the frame panel slots. Replace the panel, glue the frame together, clamp it and let it set after making certain that the frame is square and that the panel sits squarely in the frame, leaving no formerly exposed surfaces. Wipe off excess glue.

Occasionally, the loose panel cannot be removed because its frame refuses to part. In such a case, move the loose panel into one corner of its frame and squirt glue on the two exposed sides. Move the panel into the diagonally opposite corner and squirt glue along the other two exposed sides. Center the panel once again and wipe off excess glue. Here you may want to run a screwdriver under the wet cloth to get out all the new glue because it's difficult to get the glue out once it dries. Don't move anything until the panel sets.

Rotted pieces

Rotting generally means replacement of all or at least a part of the sick component. Small sections of either dry or wet rot can be repaired by cutting out the affected area and filling it with a piece of similar wood, filler, putty, wax or lacquer, depending on the size of the resulting hole and its location. Where the patch is to be large or if it is in a prominent place, it is better to fill with wood of the same species and hopefully the same vintage. See Chapter 6 for details concerning patching.

Basement flooding is a particular enemy of old furniture, and if legs and bottoms have rotted, their replacement is necessary. In the case of most bottoms and backboards, you need not be overly concerned about wood species or wood form; plywood will often do the trick. Legs, feet, columns and plinths are another matter.

The extent to which you remain faithful to the original in repairs of these components depends much on the market or sentimental value of the antique.

Newly made components should ideally match the old in wood species and age. If that proves to be impossible, you will have to depend on refinishing to cover up the look of newness. An old vanity I refinished turned out to have two new front legs after three coats of paint were removed. The new pine was much lighter than the old, a shade compensated for in refinishing. I simply put a darker stain on the two new legs, although you may be able to get away with two coats of stain on a new component, and one coat on the older piece.

Stuck furniture parts

When doors and drawers stick, look for a structural defect, particularly if the antique was acquired at a flea market or garage sale. The desk's top hinges could be the wrong size, or bent, or fastened with the wrong size or type of screw. It is even possible that the top is from another desk (a marriage), and though it is a close fit, it will need some reworking to be an exact fit.

Drawers are a common problem because they typically take so much abuse. Check for such structural problems as missing or loose drawer slides, worn drawer sides, and broken and loose drawer components. Correct these first before planing or sawing to remove wood.

Drawer slides are fastened to the interior of the chest carcass. Determine first how the other slides are fastened before you repair; then use the same materials. If a slide is completely missing, look first at the bottom of the inside of the chest or in another drawer. If you can't find one, make another by using a slide in place as your pattern. Wherever possible, nail, screw and glue back the slide, using the same old holes so that you will ensure proper placement of this part.

Drawers that are loose, broken or split should be repaired because they are the operational component of the chest. Side slide bottoms that are worn can readily be detected because the drawer front, when closed, leans inward. A perfect restoration entails glueing wood strips of the same species, age and dimension to the work slide bottoms, making a perfect rectangle out of the drawer slide. It is better, of course, to replace the entire side. That is a process for a valuable antique, however, as it entails cutting dovetails.

If the chest is not an important antique, a shortcut to drawer-side repair is to glue wider strips of anything from paint sticks to strips of plywood to the worn side slide bottom. Clamp it, but don't nail it because as the wood wears, the exposed nail heads will wear the chest carcass slide, a component which gets enough ordinary wear as it is.

Drawers that close too far into the chest carcass have their stops missing.

Typically, drawer stops are pieces of wood measuring $\frac{1}{8} \times 1 \times 2$ in. ($3.1 \times 25.4 \times 51$ mm). They are glued and nailed to the inside top of the bearer strip. Their location can be determined by the mark left by the former stop. If you cannot find the mark, place the new stop, two to a bearer strip, about 2 in. (5 cm) in from the side, and back from the front of the strip the same distance as the width of the drawer front. Glue and tack with a small brad.

Check stuck doors to see whether their hinges are tightly screwed to the carcass, whether their panel frames are coming unglued, or whether their carcass support pieces are loose and have moved. Correct any of these defects.

If drawers and doors still stick, they can be made to work better by rubbing candle wax on the moving parts. Doors can be made to fit better by cutting some wood from the hinge cuts. If doors fit too loosely, place a small piece of wood veneer or cardboard between the hinge and the cabinet carcass.

I strongly suggest that you refrain from removing wood if fixing structural defects, applying candle wax, and working with hinges fail to undo the sticking. Note whether humidity or temperature changes have any effect on the areas that stick. If no changes occur, cut if you must.

Veneer

Two important principles about veneer come to mind which I wish to pass on to you. The first is that most of us can live with more veneer problems than we think we can. An investigation of many fine antiques reveals that lifting veneer is quite common. The second principle is that extensive veneer repair is a job for an expert, though they are few in number and their services are costly.

What we will look into in this section is how you can take care of minor veneer defects. Veneer, and its close relative marquetry, are unquestionably beautiful, but are also sensitive to use and their environment. Therefore, missing, blistered, worn and lifting veneer is common on antique pieces.

Locate all veneer problems so they can be dealt with at once. After visual inspection of the surfaces, you can further identify loose veneer by tapping the surface areas: Loose veneer will sound hollow.

Decide how you are going to apply and keep pressure on the repaired areas. Clamping is one way, but for large surfaces such as the top of a round oak table, clamping will be difficult. A system of weights on pieces of wood cauls over the patch is recommended. Another approach is to wedge a pole or a 1×2-in. (2.5×5-cm) piece of soft wood between the caul and the ceiling.

Since veneer patching, repairing blisters and reglueing lifting veneer call for slightly different approaches, I'll take each one separately. First, lifting veneer because it is the easiest to fix. Carefully raise it so as to remove as much dirt, loose glue and dried glue as possible. Apply a lot of new glue under the lifted veneer and press on it with your finger to force out excessive glue, and wipe with a wet rag. Place a piece of waxed paper over the repair area, then the caul, then the pressure (clamp, weight or wedge stick). Let it set a day.

You can also break off the lifted piece of veneer and reglue it, taking care to replace it in the exact spot from which it was removed. A hot glue gun can be used to glue very small pieces of veneer. Once the glue is under the lifted piece, quickly poke additional glue underneath the veneer, followed by pressure with a stick for a few minutes until it sets. Pick away excess glue with your fingernail while the glue is still plastic.

Veneer blisters can frequently be repaired with a clothes iron, as its heat reactivates the old glue underneath the veneer. Place waxed paper over the blister, then a folded rag over the paper. Place a hot iron on the cloth for a few seconds and check to see if the blister is flat. If it is, clamp it by placing a caul over the waxed paper. If the blister is still there, apply more heat. If repeated attempts at this procedure fail, it will be necessary to put new glue into the blister.

You can get new glue into the blister by slitting the blister with a sharp razor blade, following a grain line. Push down one side of the blister and push glue into the raised other side with a sharp, small knife; do the same for the other side. Squeeze out excess glue, place waxed paper, caul and pressure over the repair, and let set overnight.

Replacing veneer may also be required because of badly damaged lifted pieces or damaged blistered areas. You must first square the sides of the damaged area. Use a steel rule and a sharp razor blade (a veneer knife is even better), and cut a replacement veneer patch to fit the opening. For exact fitting, sand the edge of the veneer replacement piece, laid flat on your bench top, with 120 grade sandpaper. Be sure the patch fits before applying glue to both patch and exposed core. Wipe excess glue, cover with waxed paper, caul, apply pressure and let set.

Look over your antique piece for a veneer area where removal of a small piece won't be noticed, such as a kneehole area of a desk, the inside of a cabinet door or an unneeded table leaf.

Places in which you can buy veneer exist in every large city. You may have to buy a very large quantity of veneer to get a very small piece, though. Another disadvantage is that matching colors, grains and thickness of modern veneer to that of an antique may be difficult. Older, thicker veneers can often be matched by glueing several layers of modern veneers. Color differences can be satisfactorily matched by touching up the veneer patch later in the refinishing process.

Warpage

Occasional tabletops and plant tabletops that are warped are quite common illnesses among antiques. Cabinet doors come in a close second. Interestingly enough, it is moisture that caused the warping, and it is moisture that will take it out. All the finish from the warped item must be removed with paint-and-varnish remover because old finish prevents moisture absorption. After removing the varnish, place a wet Turkish towel on a flat cement floor; use more towels if working with a large piece of furniture. Separate the tabletop from the rest of the table, and place the tabletop on the wet towel, concave surface down. Place heavy weights, such as several concrete blocks, on the top. In a day or so, the top will appear flat.

Step two is to move the warped top, panel or shelf off the towel. Remove the towel and replace the repair on the same spot on the floor, which by now is also wet. Let it set there a day so it can begin to dry out. In step three, flip the tabletop, putting what was the convex side down under the weight. On the third day, move the repair to a dry spot, still under weights. Finally, let it sit on a wooden bench top (assuming it is flat) for several days so it can completely dry, and keep flipping it.

After you're certain the component is dry, quickly assemble it to the rest of the antique piece and complete its restoration. Strip off the rest of the pieces, finish and then refinish them before the top begins to absorb the wrong kind of moisture in its unsealed state.

This is a very good technique to master because with this knowledge you will be able to pick up some real bargains and restore them.

Missing antique furniture parts

If your furniture is missing some of its parts, you can buy and/or make the missing parts. Stretchers, plain spindles and even round chair legs can be made simply from wooden dowels purchased in your local hardware store or lumberyard. In order to borrow, you may have to destroy several other pieces. For example, you may have to buy six chairs to get enough parts to have four good ones. Finally, you can buy some missing parts, such as table leaves, particularly for table widths of 44 in. (112 cm) and 48 in. (122 cm).

Dowels are the basic material for turned parts. If the missing component is plain, your task is simple. Just buy a new dowel close to the size you need and cut it to its correct length, taking into consideration the distance it will have to go in its respective stretcher or spindle holes. Then trim the ends of the piece a little with a rasp so it will fit properly. Glue it, insert it, and clamp if possible.

If the spindle or stretcher has a pattern to it, turning the dowel on a lathe is the ideal way to copy the design. Since the average nonprofessional restorer does not have a lathe, the turnings can be duplicated with a wood rasp instead. In this instance, keep the dowel longer than needed to give you something to grasp. Make a U-shaped cut in a piece of one-by-two, place the one-by-two in a vise and let one end of the dowel rest in the U-cut. Mark the cuts on the dowel, and make the design cuts with a rasp while turning the dowel with your free hand. When you're through with the rasp, sand everything smooth, starting with rough sandpaper and ending with smooth. You'll find that this process takes some time.

Often various mouldings are missing from tops of wardrobes, under desk tops and at the base of pieces. Many of these mouldings can be carved, made with a router or with an antique moulding plane. Also, you can often buy pine, birch or oak moulding in lumberyards and then cut and glue up several pieces to give you the configuration you want. Another source of such mouldings is an architectural trim-and-moulding firm that caters to old-house restorers. Many large cities have such places where old wood can be bought.

As noted, you may have to buy a piece of furniture or two and dismantle it to get replacement parts. A difficult part to replace is the bentwood hip-hugger, or the back brace on a Golden Oak chair. A missing pressed-back is still more difficult to replace. Rather than try carving one, I suggest you buy a chair and use it for replacement parts.

Another vexing problem is the missing table leaf or leaves. It seems that in olden times many folks misplaced their boards, forgot to take them when they moved, or used them to construct lovely hardwood shelves. You will just have to search the flea markets and try to talk a dealer out of some of his table boards.

Of course, a thorough search of the premises, including barns and the homes of relatives, may turn up just what you want. Also check painted items in the cellar such as shelves used for canned goods. Finally, new oak may have to be the solution. Since extended tables often are covered with a tablecloth, even plywood might suffice.

Gouges and holes

Although the patching of most gouges and holes will be covered in detail in Chapter 6, those of a more serious nature will be discussed here. One serious defect is a hole in a veneer surface. The hole itself can be filled with anything, so long as veneer is placed over the top surface.

Larger holes and round holes can best be filled with a large diameter dowel, pole section or even a piece of a broom handle. I would enlarge the hole slightly so that the patch piece fits, since it's easier to drill a new hole than to reduce the size of a dowel.

A common hole in desk drawer fronts is found where the lock has been removed. While I suggest that the center desk drawer or rolltop lock be replaced for practical as well as aesthetic reasons, the lock holes on other drawer fronts can be patched. For this I usually use maple dowels and try to line up the grain so it goes with the pores of oak, the material from which old desks are typically made. Carefully sand the dowel end that will be exposed.

If the hole in a tabletop or chest of drawers is round and large enough, a dowel is a suitable fill. As the dowel end will take stain and sealer differently than the top, a little pretesting for proper color match is advisable. For critical fills, however, nothing beats using the same wood species. You can cut small circles, sand them perfectly round and smooth, and glue them in place.

When it comes to gouge problems, my feeling as a professional restorer is that *some* gouges belong in the surface of an antique piece. They are called "care marks" and are a testimony to the use that has been given a particular piece over time.

The ways to remove unsightly gouges are to sand, fill and touch up. Sanding will not only remove your gouges, but it will also remove your wood, creating a dished area. Sanding also lightens wood in the adjacent surface areas and consequently requires either more refinishing work or the sanding of the entire surface. Despite its dangers, sanding is a good way to remove some shallow gouges.

Another approach is to fill the gouge. While the techniques of filling will be covered later (Chapter 6), filling is a good approach to take when the gouge is deep since it takes depth to hold the fill.

A third approach is to touch up the gouge mark. Touch-up has the distinct advantage of covering up much of the gouge, especially if it is a shallow one, as many cigarette burns are. But more on this later (Chapter 6).

Minor Repair Problems

WOOD SCREWS. Often wood screws will no longer hold the hinge, the foot caster or the pull. The reason for its reduced or nonexistent holding power is that the threads cut by the screw in the wood have worn out or have disappeared. You can give the wood screw new life by inserting the tip of a wooden toothpick covered with glue into the old screw hole. If more filler is needed, use still another toothpick and then replace the screw.

GLUE REPAIRS THAT KEEP SEPARATING. Repairs that keep separating, dowels that continually come out, veneer that keeps lifting, and dovetail joints that won't stay together are usually a waste of time to try to repair again. Here you should cut away enough wood to ensure only raw wood remains, and glue in new pieces, such as corewood, dowels and parts of a joint; you can then make the assembly.

MIRRORS. Old mirrors lose their silver; mercury mirrors lose their mercury. In the restoration of an antique, there is often the decision to make whether or not to restore the mirror, buy a replacement mirror or just let things be. Defective mercury mirrors cannot be restored. The condition of the mirror in part determines whether it should be replaced; but keep in mind that replacement often lowers the market value of a particularly fine antique.

Silvered mirrors can be resilvered, usually for nominal costs. Bevelled mirrors are increasingly more expensive to obtain, so you may want to get a bevelled mirror resilvered. Before you do that, however, check to see if there are any surface scratches on it. Such scratches cannot be removed in the resilvering process and will mitigate its restoration.

If the mirror is an ordinary, nonbevelled one, it pays to replace it, especially if it is functionally useless.

Frank Lloyd Wright Dining Suite

To sum up this chapter on repair of antique and very valuable furniture, it is perhaps relevant to tell you about the repairs I made on the Frank Lloyd Wright Family dining suite (c. 1890) for the Frank Lloyd Wright Home and Studio Foundation in Oak Park, Illinois.

The six side chairs, a child's high chair and the dining table were all designed by Wright, although the table is not originally from this room. The chairs were originally a sort of Jacobean/Golden Oak/Gothic design and were later modified under Wright's directions to conform to the Mission Oak style that he adopted and designed for his prairie houses.

All the chair components are made of solid oak and are assembled with dowel joints. Typical of furniture prior to 1910 or so, the dowels have no glue grooves turned in them. While the chair spindles are now square Mission Oak style, the original ones were turned spindles that were cut off both at the top rail and the crossbar. A thin strip of moulding was then glued over original dowel holes to cover them. Modification of the chairs also entailed round ball finials to replace the elaborate Victorian ones originally there, a curved piece of oak fastened to the rear legs, and a parallel cut made in the front of each, not at all Mission style.

Chair repair consisted of completely dismantling the piece since the old glue had dried out. Chair spindles were kept in their same original order and in their same direction when removed. The chairs were disassembled by using a hammer and mallet to start the separation; two crowbars were used so as to provide even upward pressure when applied to the opening, and separation continued. All spindles were removed by hand since they were so loose in their dowel holes.

Some parts were difficult to separate, and I broke one back-upright in the process. Many parts were well dowelled; for example, the top rail is connected to the back upright with four dowels at each side.

All dowels were tested to see if the end remaining in a given component was tight. Both dowels and dowel holes were then cleaned of old glue. The backs of

Two Frank Lloyd Wright chairs before refinishing and reupholstering. They are dark and dirty from nearly 80 years of use and previous "handyman" refinishing.

the chairs were glued first, with spindles being assembled into the top rail and crossbar. The back-uprights were fastened to the rail and bar. This was clamped and set overnight. The side rails and assembled H-stretchers were assembled into the front legs and the entire subassembly connected to the back-uprights and legs, set on the flat floor, checked for squareness, and clamped. Components were first assembled with hand pressure once all the dowels were lined up, and they were tapped together with a mallet on a wood scrap to prevent hammer marks. Pipe clamps pulled the entire assembly completely together and held it.

The dining table was 7 ft. (2.1 m) long. All seven top boards had separated as had most of the hollow box legs. The channels connecting the legs had also separated, so disassembly was not a challenge. What was difficult about this piece was reglueing the top boards. I used three 5-ft. (1.5-m) pipe clamps to pull the boards and their eight dowels together. After assembly, the surfaces of several boards on one side did not line up, despite the fact that the original dowel holes were used. This probably resulted because the top had been allowed to deteriorate and top boards had been separated for some time, thus warping out of alignment.

The efficacy of synthetic glue was demonstrated in this instance. I was able to separate the unsatisfactory boards, plug the dowel holes and drill new ones to bring about top-surface alignment. A dowel jig was used so that perfect alignment could be facilitated.

After the top was assembled, I screwed three poplar strips to the underneath side of the top: one at each end and one in the middle. This arrangement began to fail three years later as some boards began to separate. I again separated the top, cleaned off the old glue, and replaced everything. This time, however, plywood strips were glued to the underside, screwed and clamped. This time it will hold!

3   *Stripping Furniture*

When stripping antique furniture, it is necessary to remove all of the old finish from the wood surface in order to achieve a really satisfactory and professional restoration job. Techniques and products which call for "schmossing" around the old finish, or amalgamation or rearrangement of the finish, come off second best in my opinion. This is because stripping is not an end in itself; it leads to restoration, and the better the furniture surface preparation, the better the finished piece will look. Removal of the original finish of an antique clearly reduces its value, so you will want to carefully consider this phase of restoration. Consider whether the piece already has another restorer's finish on it; if it does, you can proceed to strip the piece. If the acquisition finish is original, consider its condition. Has it unduly darkened with age due to moisture absorption by the shellac finish? Has the paint and most of the pattern worn off your Pennsylvania chest of drawers? Has your rolltop desk acquired an alligatored-varnish finish? If so, it needs to be stripped and refinished.

I guess that the borderline "Should-I-strip-or-shouldn't-I" situations are the most difficult to resolve. If that is your problem, perhaps you should first choose the cleaning alternative and see if that solves your finish problem.

The Cleaning Alternative

At times all your antique furniture piece needs is a very thorough cleaning to restore its beauty. Reflect for a moment how dirty modern furniture gets in a year. Then multiply that by 100 or 150 years' worth of dirt, and you have a goodly layer, as well as waxes and polishes, deposited on the surface. Finally, if the item you intend to restore has been in storage for any length of time, it has acquired a more grimy patina, so try cleaning it if the present finish has possibilities.

As water is the enemy of all wood, use as little as possible. I recommend an oil soap be used exactly as directed, and detergent should not be used at all.

Hand-Stripping vs. Dip or Spray

In general, hand-stripping of antique furniture is recommended, though it is more tedious than other stripping techniques. Dip-stripping by commercial houses, in my opinion, is reserved for pieces of little value, pieces with many coats of paint on them, or for architectural items like shutters. Spray-stripping, I am told, is sort of in between these two procedures, and it is supposed to be less damaging because it exposes the wood to much less moisture.

Hand-stripping is generally better because it uses much less water and reduces the danger of damage. The problem with water is that it not only softens and removes glue, but excessive exposure to water caused by long soaking can warp wood and cause it to split when it is later left to dry out. Finally, the chemical used by commercial dippers raises the grain, at times making it look like a dried sponge when you get the piece back.

If you believe that water is going to be a problem due to very fine veneer or marquetry, you need use none in hand-stripping. There are strippers which call for sanding to remove the remaining dried residue, and no water damage is possible. While I always use a water-soluble stripper, I am very careful about the quantity of water I use, and I quickly dry pieces after the stripping process.

How to Strip

Tools and materials

The necessary tools are simple and inexpensive, the exception being the electric paint remover, an optional tool. First and foremost is the putty knife, both the wide and the narrow variety, used for scooping off the dissolved finish residue. A bevelled straight chisel that's 1 in. (2.5 cm) wide is a very handy tool for getting in corners. Stripper is applied with a brush; highly recommended is an older China bristle, tapered brush that's 2–3 in. (51–76 mm) wide. Don't waste your time working with a beat-up, narrow, variety-store brush.

Wire brushes, both steel and brass, are also helpful. They save time and steel wool. Steel wool, of course, either number 1 or number 2, works well. You'll also need two large pails for holding water, and a smaller one to hold the stripper container. Both should be metal. I keep the stripper in a 3-lb. (1.4-kg) peanut butter jar and carry that around in a small 4-qt. (3.8-L) metal pail. Two water pails work better than one because they reduce your trips to the faucet for clean water and your trips outside to dump the dirty water.

The electric paint remover deserves some mention because it is an optional tool for removing heavy paint layers from flat furniture surfaces. Areas where it is especially useful are cabinet or cupboard shelves, the sides of case goods and flat fronts, and the tops and interiors of case goods. Because of the danger of scorching wood, this tool should not be used on lightly painted or curved and turned surfaces. Also, if the paint has been applied directly over raw wood, you should not use this tool.

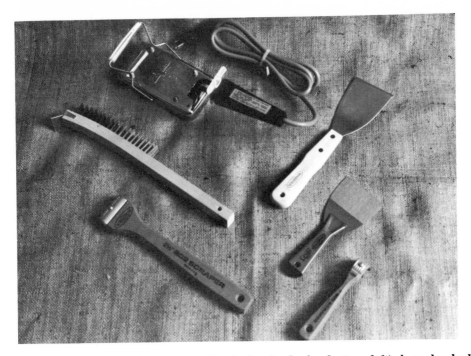

Tools used in the stripping process (clockwise, beginning bottom left): large hooked scraper, wire brush, electric paint remover, large scraper, wide putty knife and a small hooked scraper.

As with most craft work, one should use as large a tool as is necessary to do the job. The "toothpick" approach to stripping should be avoided unless you really enjoy this sort of activity and want to lengthen the project. I depend heavily on the 3-in. (7.6-cm) putty knife, a clean, wide stripper application brush and a long-handled wire brush.

The principal material in stripping, of course, is the chemical stripper. While some of the old-timers in the trade have homemade concoctions, the average person will do best by buying a commercial product, preferably by the gallon. These compounds all contain methylene chloride that's suspended in an agent that prevents the drying of the active agent.

Other materials include towels and rags. Since I use old bath towels extensively and cut them into halves or thirds, the cut edges have been sewn to prevent unravelling. As water-soluble strippers enable towels and rags to be washed and, therefore, recycled, I rarely get them too dirty.

General stripping tips

Before we get into the actual stripping process, we should look at some general tips, which I have acquired over the years.

1. Once you start to strip an antique, complete it that day, being sure to give yourself plenty of time for first projects. Certainly, never let the stripper dry anywhere. However, if you cannot finish your project in one day, finish scraping old finished loosened by stripper and clean that area thoroughly with steel wool.

2. Do your stripping at a comfortable work height. I have several portable benches and tables of different heights, making it unusual for me to do any work on the floor. Stripping furniture on the floor is not only hard on your back, but it also slows you down and makes for an unsatisfactory job. The feet and bottoms of pieces in particular suffer from floor-level stripping.

3. While you're stripping, get *all* of the old finish out at that time. While some corner aggregates can be easily scraped out when dried, most of such residue must be heavily scraped or sanded off later, a much more difficult task than stripping.

4. Work with clean materials: brush, rags and stripper. You can keep the stripper clean by (a) stopping to brush on more stripper when the brush appears to be picking up dissolved residue, (b) working with a smaller amount of stripper at a time, (c) dumping the stripper when it appears to be getting very thin and discolored, and (d) cleaning out your brush occasionally with newspaper.

5. Having music to listen to while stripping is great motivation. I carry my cassette recorder with me when working away from my shops and keep a portable stereo in each shop.

Stripping precautions

PREPARATIONS. Pick a well-ventilated and well-lit area in which to do your stripping; I work outdoors in the country when the weather is friendly. If your floor can be damaged by stripping, cover it with heavy plastic, and then with at least three layers of newspapers. As the paper gets dirty with the old finish and stripper, lay more on the sticky spots rather than pick up the debris-covered layers. This will result in a greater thickness that will later absorb the water used in the washing process. Cover anything that can possibly be damaged by paint-and-varnish remover, including plastic.

PRECAUTIONS. Methylene chloride, an active agent in strippers, is toxic; therefore, you should keep your windows and doors open, even in winter when working with stripping solution. I usually work with a large fan to circulate the air. Besides its toxic nature, this chemical is hard on your skin and eyes; so cover your arms, wear neoprene gloves, glasses made of glass (*not* plastic), and work in your grubbiest jeans. If you should splash any stripper on your face or in your eyes, immediately wash it off. Do not let stripper collect in any quantity on clothing that is in direct contact with your skin because it will burn the area, which will take several weeks to heal. It can be nasty stuff; I have the scars to prove it.

Once you've completed the stripping job, move the piece to another area to dry and immediately pick up the wet and dirty newspaper. I do this by rolling it, flattening it by standing on it, and packing it into a large plastic yard bag.

Clean your brush by washing it in strong laundry detergent and then rinse it off. Wire brushes and pails can be cleaned in the same manner. Soak towels in a pail of hot detergent water if they're not absolutely filthy; they can then be washed and recycled. Dump all rinse water outside in the street-curb sewer drain if you live in the city, or on the ground in the country. While the residue doesn't seem to hurt trees or plants, it can clog plumbing.

How to strip various finishes

It is possible to strip various old finishes with different solvents at times. Different finishes require slightly different techniques, even when the same solvent is used. In this section we'll take a close look at shellac, lacquer, varnish and paint.

SHELLAC. You may want to consider stripping old shellac by using denatured alcohol. Test first to see if the present finish is shellac, and then apply denatured alcohol with a brush, working a small area first and then a larger one as you get the feel of the piece and its finish. If the shellac is thick, you can scrape it off with your putty knife; otherwise, wipe it off with steel wool.

As the old finish thins down, begin to remove it with steel wool, rotating the pad so that a clean surface is working for you. Dip the steel wool in alcohol and wipe the surface. Finally, wipe the piece with a rag that's been dipped in alcohol. Now is the time to get in corners, carvings, scrolls and incised lines. Poke your chisel into the alcohol-soaked rag and clean out corners, along panels and their frames, and through the incised lines of your Eastlake piece. Dry everything with a clean cloth. If the piece still feels sticky, use some more alcohol until that feeling is gone.

Paint-and-varnish remover (stripper) works well on shellacked finishes; in fact, it works especially quickly and efficiently because shellac is not a tough finish. To use stripper on shellac, follow the directions under "varnish" on the next page.

LACQUER. All contemporary furniture has been finished with lacquer unless, of course, it is painted. You can remove lacquer by applying lacquer thinner. First test to see if your piece has a lacquer finish; if it does, follow the directions for stripping shellac with alcohol. As with stripper, you will want to provide plenty of ventilation for both lacquer thinner and alcohol.

Chemical stripper is brushed onto only half of the tabletop at one time. Author is wearing gloves and is using a 2-in. (5cm) - wide brush that has been well cleaned. Stripper is kept in a large glass jar and carried in a convenient-sized metal pail. Stripper should be brushed on the surface and not worked into the wood.

VARNISH. The only solvent that will remove varnish is paint-and-varnish remover. Although varnish was undoubtedly applied as the initial finish on your antique, it is the most likely finish you will find on it because of the work of previous restorers or handymen. Some pieces I have stripped have had four or five coats of varnish on them; they were so thick you could almost peel them off.

To strip varnish, brush the stripper on a suitable work area so that the entire top of a small chest or an occasional tabletop is covered. Repeat the process, using generous amounts of stripper. Under normal conditions the old finish should start to bubble when it is ready to be scraped off. As you are working over plenty of newspaper, scrape the residue directly onto the paper. If no bubbling occurs, scrape off what has dissolved.

Repeat this process several times until none of the old finish is left on the surfaces, cleaning the last application with steel wool. Lay on one more coat of stripper and wash it off with warm water. For hard woods, a new wire brush moved only in the direction of the grain will really clean the grain. For soft woods, use steel wool with the water; clean off hard woods with steel wool after using the wire brush. Rinse all surfaces with a wet Turkish towel (preferably the size of a hand towel), and dry with a clean, dry towel. Place the piece where it can dry quickly, but avoid extreme heat or sunlight.

If there is too much varnish on the piece it will not bubble, but will merely get viscous. Scrape off the material and keep repeating this activity until the wash step. Hot, dry conditions will cause the solvent to dry quickly, necessitating the stripping of a smaller area at a time. Be sure to overlay your stripping when cleaning small areas, especially when a large tabletop is involved.

For illustration purposes, the stripper was scraped off before complete soaking so as to show some of the old varnish coming off. The scraper is a flexible 3-in. (7.5-cm) putty knife. Old finish is scraped onto newspaper that covers the floor and then covered with additional newspaper.

How do you know when the piece is completely stripped? Well, there is an evenness to the stripped wood color and no shine to any portion. The wood color will probably be darker than it originally was due to stain, if any, and to its age. While old wood will always be a different color than new wood, stripped wood generally looks pinker, whiter or lighter than before it was stripped. Since it is difficult to tell exactly when a piece has been adequately stripped, I suggest that you initially overstrip until experience tells you when is the right time to quit.

PAINT. Some very valuable old pieces will lose much of their value when their painted patina is removed. If the paint that covers your antique is not the original coat, and this is most likely the case, it has probably been applied over a sealed surface. Good! That means this old finish can be removed much more easily and satisfactorily than paint applied over raw (unsealed) wood.

To remove paint (the most difficult finish to strip), brush the stripper on the surface, as you would varnish remover. Again, look for bubbling. While the same process as that for varnish should be used, it may be necessary to repeat applications a few more times. Unlike varnish, stripper should be allowed to set and soak.

A third application of stripper is necessary for this table, the last for this particular job.

It is faster and you use less stripper in the long run if you keep brushing on more stripper before your first scraping. Stripper generally soaks through to the wood if enough material is used and enough time is allowed. An exception is latex paint, which flakes off when stripper is applied and makes soaking impossible.

You know when you're through stripping because the grain stands out clearly, and there is no visible trace of paint pigment. If, however, repeated applications and removals of stripper seem to result in the same surface appearance, go into the wash process and dry off the piece. You're through stripping; sanding might remove some of the remaining pigment. It is more than likely that some pigment will remain, causing your refinishing job to be less than satisfactory.

Paint gets into corners, cracks and designs, and at times is impossible to get out. One solution to this problem is wire brushing. Be careful when going against the grain and when cleaning soft woods because the solvent and water soften the wood, making the brush a destructive weapon if not used correctly.

The embossed, decorative tabletop edge is being cleaned with a wire brush. The wash application of stripper is then made (not shown), making only two applications of stripper necessary for this table.

Another solution to the problem of paint in recessed areas and corners is to leave it there and to touch up such spots later. Colored lacquer or paint the color of the finished piece can be successfully used to cover up such defects after the sealing step in the refinishing process. For more information on touch-up, see Chapter 6.

SANDING AND SCRAPING. This is an alternative to stripping which should not be used as a main finish removal technique. Some wood is removed along with the finish in this technique, and old finishes need a chemical for effective removal.

A long-handled wire brush will clean out remaining residue from the pores and will not scratch hard woods such as oak *if* it is worked *with* the grain.

Since using special cutting tools to strip paint can damage wood, I do not recommend such a procedure. However, the exception is where there is very little material to remove and you plan to repaint the piece; thus, a plain, Cottage-style storage chest with worn and flaking paint would qualify for scraping and sanding.

What stripping reveals

Removing the old finish from an antique usually reveals a fairly clean surface, a lovely color and sometimes a beautiful wood grain. But sometimes, to your surprise, you may instead uncover old plant rings, ink spills, holes filled with plaster, and errors in finishing. It is at a time like this that you wish you had let the piece be!

If the surface of the piece is a real disaster, you have several ways of dealing with it. One, repaint it; so as not to have worked in vain, however, lay on a more suitable color. Two, sanding the imperfections (see Chapter 4). Three, if the defects revealed are minimal, touch-up may work (see Chapter 6).

Stripping Certain Antiques

So far I have presented some tips on stripping and have indicated how stripping the more common finishes found on antique and old furniture is to be done. In this section, I'm going to relate my favorite ways of stripping certain antique furniture pieces. These techniques should make your task much simpler.

Tables

Let's start with the drop leaf and its cousin, the gateleg. Both have a drop leaf, the underside of which should also be refinished. At first I stripped a drop-leaf table on a worktable that was 14 in. (35 cm) high, but I still had to practically stand on my head to get underneath the drop leaf. For the gateleg, often a spool-turned model, the legs and crossbars were difficult to do. Then one day I decided to experiment by turning the table upside down on a higher worktable, and strip both the legs and the underside of the drop leaf in a much more work-accessible position.

I first stripped the legs of the drop-leaf table, carefully covering the underside not slated for stripping. Then the underside of the drop leaves were stripped. Finally, I righted the table, stood it on paper on the floor and stripped the top. This system works well for occasional tables, too.

In general, though, it's better to strip the tabletop first: you don't slop up the stripped legs with the residue from the top. In the case of Victorian height tables, I strip the top first while the piece is on the floor, then lift it to a workbench and strip the legs and crossbars, if any.

It is helpful to have your stripping bench located so that you can walk around

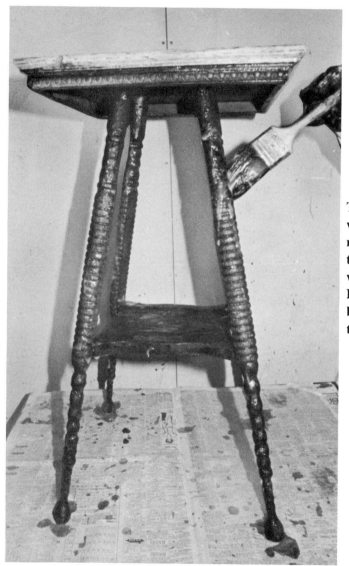

The legs of the table were wiped dry with newspaper, and the table was elevated to worktable height. Here, the stripper is being brushed into the leg turnings.

it as you work. If possible, have lighting on all four sides; you can do this by getting small reflectorlike extension lights that clamp on to anything.

Round oak tables are deceptively simple to strip; don't let their size scare you! Start with the leaves and strip them on the tabletop, first laying an open plastic lawn bag on the tabletop and covering it with newspaper. Strip half the top at a time, including the skirt. Separate the halves slightly and be sure to clean residue from that opening, using steel wool. Leave the top on its base even if it is unscrewed. Use the putty knife for removing large quantities of residue, then wire-brush the surfaces by going with the grain all the way across a half. Follow the brush with steel wool, then give the top the wash application, and dry.

Since such a large table base is awkward to reach, it is helpful to get it up on concrete blocks, or even a low worktable. A particularly difficult stripping job, entailing the removal of the base, should also be done on a worktable. Such extension bases often have claw feet. The best tool for getting old finish out of claw feet that I've found is the wire brush.

Large rectangular tables often have too large a top surface to strip at one time without drying out a lot of stripper. You can divide the top into portions and work a smaller area, while slightly overlapping the previously stripped one, especially in the wash step.

The left half of this tabletop has been stripped of old finish.

Chairs

Whereas tables seem difficult to strip and turn out to be simple, the opposite is true with chairs.

In stripping finish from a chair, it is best to start with the upper half and the seat. Do this work with the piece either on the floor or on a low worktable. Strip the bottom half with the chair at counter height. To get the feet perfectly stripped, you may want to turn the chair over and rest it on a workbench, either on its back or on its seat.

Stripping turnings on chair-back spindles, legs, arms and almost everywhere on platform rockers takes some effort. It is best to brush on the stripper and let it set, but be sure to keep it wet. Careful use of a wire brush, working it across the groove part of the turning, is good, but watch out for scratching the bulbs. When using a Turkish towel for rinsing and drying, work it back and forth in and round the turnings. Note where spindles and stretchers connect with other components specifically, as a buildup of old finish may be found there.

Pressed-back chairs, of course, feature a "carved" top rail. This recessed area, a natural catcher of old finishes, makes removal of such finishes, especially paint, difficult. It is a good idea to lay the chair on a bench so the back is horizontal. Brush in lots of stripper, allowing it time to really soak into the design. Remove residue with a wire brush, taking care not to scratch the wood.

Beds

Since bed sideboards are simple, straight pieces, start your stripping with them to get the feel for the job. Tall headboards can best be handled when leaned against a wall. Besides, you generally have to refinish only one side. Footboards, however, must be stripped on two sides. Stand them against a wall and do one side at a time, although short footboards can be placed on a worktable and stripped one side at a time. The best method, however, is to set up the bed in your work area and strip it as it would ordinarily be positioned. Put down plenty of newspaper, preferably over plastic sheets.

Eastlake Victorian headboards, like all pieces in this style, have incised lines and machine-carved geometric designs: leafs, scrolls and even flowers. For a good finishing job, remove all the old finish from these recessed areas. Really soak the designs with stripper. Carefully use a wire brush to clean out residue from carved parts and places where panels meet; be especially careful if the wood is soft. While you may have to dig out some residue, remember that you can always touch up hard-to-get-at areas later.

Murphy beds, a rather rare item, are folding beds from the late Victorian period that collapse into a case that looks a lot like a large cabinet or chest of drawers, complete with fake pulls. To strip one, you must work both the outside and the underneath side, as well as the inside. Open the bed and remove the spring and the entire box section that holds the springs. Strip the inside of the case and the inside of the box-spring section. After drying that, fold it back in the case and strip all exterior components. Be sure to remove finish from all parts which will show when the bed is being used.

Spool-turned beds, like all spool-turned pieces, are best stripped when working on all sides of the given component at once. I usually start by stripping the top rail. I then go from left to right on the vertical rails and spindles, soaking and stripping as many at a time as possible under the particular weather conditions that day. While I make use of the steel wire brush, you may want to use the more gentle plastic-bristle brush.

Brushes should be kept unclogged for efficient stripping: Scrape them on a sharp paint scraper, brush them together, or wash them out and dry them quickly in the sunlight. I usually work with about a dozen brushes at a time, permitting cleaning and drying. Keep turning your steel wool pad and dispose of it when it appears full, because an overworked pad has stopped working for you. Finally, let the stripper do the work. Use a lot of it, and let it soak.

The main difficulties with stripping Renaissance Victorian head and footboards are their mouldings and applied reliefs. Residue stuck around and inside this decor must be soaked out with lots of stripper. The remaining small amount of residue can usually be removed after the rinse and drying steps. At that point, take a dry rag that's wrapped around a large poking tool (such as your bevelled chisel, a butcher knife or a large ice pick) and clean out the remainder. Do not smear adjacent clean areas. It's a lot easier to remove the residue when it's damp than when it's wet or dry. For hardwood pieces, I often use a dry wire brush or clean steel wool pad to clean out such residue after everything has dried.

Chests and sideboards

Chests of drawers and sideboards have so much in common that they will be detailed together. With these pieces, it is best to first strip the drawers because they are the easiest and they give you a feel for the finish and the wood you'll be working with. Remove the drawer pulls, if possible, and, of course, the drawers. If the carcass is a convenient work height, cover its top and strip the drawers on it. Usually, stripping the front is sufficient. Ugly interiors may cause you to want to strip them, too, but I must warn you that it may be the toughest part of the job, especially if paint has been applied over raw wood.

If there is a mirror, strip it next, in place if it is attached or on the carcass top if it has been detached. Note if old finish has seeped behind the mirror frame on the glass. If this is unsightly, you will have to take the mirror out of its frame in order to clean it. Mirror frames are often a lot easier to handle without their mirrors. Still another benefit to removing the mirror is that you will have an opportunity to clean the back of the mirror.

After stripping the carcass by starting with the top, catching all the mouldings and grooves, as well as the handkerchief drawers, if any, do the sides and the chest front. You may want to place the piece on a 14-in. (35-cm) worktable in an upright position, or you may want to tip the carcass on its side while doing the other side and tip it on its back while stripping the front. When stripping the carcass front, pay particular attention to front uprights and bearer strips, and be sure any old finish there will not be visible when the drawers are in place.

Both metal and wooden pulls that you were able to remove from the drawer fronts should be stripped by letting them soak in a container of stripper until the paint on them literally falls off. Put the pulls in a bucket of hot water, swish everything around, clean a little with steel wool, rinse and dry. Be careful not to lose the nuts or screws on these pieces, as they are usually difficult to replace.

Upholstered furniture

Suppose you want to strip the wood trim on a Victorian medallion sofa and the velvet upholstery is still perfectly good? How should you go about it?

Start by cutting several pieces of heavy drop-cloth-variety plastic to fit the contours of this piece. Use several because it is easier than forcing one to fit, and tape them together on the piece with masking tape. Cut close to any arms and back supports, leaving a little upholstery fabric exposed. Hold the plastic in place with wide masking tape, keeping the tape right up against any wood to be stripped. It may be necessary to put several pieces of tape in one spot to prevent any stripper or residue from getting on the fabric. Lay newspaper on the seat to absorb excessive stripper and to provide a place for your pail and steel wool pads.

When brushing on the stripper, start at the back top rail and work your way down, making sure to apply a very limited amount of stripper at a time so as to prevent seepage. Use an old rag to mop up excess. Rinse, using a damp rag rather than a wet one.

In the cleanup, dispose of the paper. With a damp rag, wipe around each opening, cleaning up the plastic and masking tape. Carefully pull up the tape and the plastic, being ready to prevent any residue from getting on the fabric. Be sure to clean up immediately when through stripping. This is one job you shouldn't let sit unfinished overnight, or you may wind up having to do an upholstery job as well as a refinishing one. Finally, I feel that it is better to leave some wood unstripped than to get stripper on the upholstery; what you miss you'll simply have to remove later by scraping and sanding.

Pianos

Piano cases are not particularly difficult to restore, but piano workings are another matter to be left to professionals! The problems with pianos are that they're heavy—therefore their mobility is difficult—and keyboards and other nonwood items need protection from stripper.

As to mobility, the piece can often be restored in the room where it is normally kept. You can protect both walls and carpeting with plastic drop cloths. If this is impossible, you will have to get piano movers to put the piece in your garage or barn where you can refinish it, and then have it moved back (it's still a lot cheaper doing it that way than sending it out to a professional restorer).

Keyboards can be heavily taped and care can be exercised in applying stripper, removing and rinsing it. Another tip to remember is to remove as many pieces as you can for the restoration process. Tops, covers and music racks all come off. For the actual stripping of a piano, I suggest that you follow the hints presented up to this point: A piano is a lot like a chest of drawers, sideboard or table, only bigger and heavier. A minor problem, however, is the insignia or label, indicating who made the piece. If the firm is still in business you might be able to get a new label once the old one is stripped off.

Wardrobes

Bulk is a central problem when refinishing most wardrobes, as it is with pianos. It might be helpful to take large wardrobes apart for stripping, perhaps even re-finishing. Don't forget to strip and refinish both sides of the doors, the custom with all cabinets. If the interior is poorly finished, you may want to strip it as well.

Related to wardrobes are all sorts of cabinets from jelly cupboards to pie safes to Dutch kitchens. In contrast to most wardrobes (which were designed for the bedroom and frequently matched beds and chests), these cupboards are often more functional and more cheaply made and finished. Softer woods then employed really absorbed the old finish, making the piece more difficult to strip.

The raw poplar or pine of some Dutch kitchens was painted over, ruling out a perfect restoration. Pie safes typically have a tin side panel arrangement that bears punctured designs. Subsequent painting of the tin completely covered the holes, and the softness of tin precludes the use of a wire brush. Considerable soaking by stripper combined with "hair pin" paint removal, may be necessary.

Because most pie safes and jelly cupboards are constructed of light, thin wood, they can be easily maneuvered. Set your pie safe on one side while you strip the other, and lay it on its back on a low table to strip the front. Take the old finish off the top at this point to avoid doing that job from a ladder at a later time. Strip the insides of the doors now, too, if they require it.

57

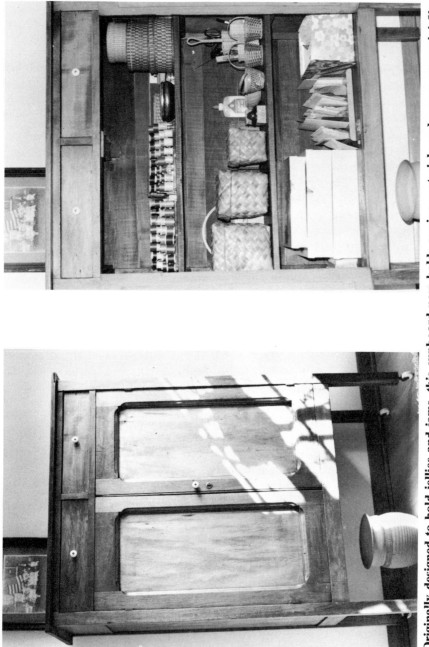

Originally designed to hold jellies and jams, this cupboard now holds sewing materials and serves as a mini file cabinet.

Desks

The rolltop desk is the most difficult model you will encounter, primarily because of the rolltop itself. Ordinary flat-top desks have much in common with chests. The exception is the kneehole between the pedestals. Access to it may be gained either by raising the desk, flipping the desk over after stripping the top, or by crawling under the desk on your hands and knees.

A rolltop desk I recently restored was a turn-of-the-century piece. I removed the rolltop, stripped the wood slats of their old finish, soaked off the old canvas backing, and scraped the old glue from the wooden surfaces. It was unusual to find that some handyman had glued canvas over the old canvas, making removal of two layers necessary. To prevent the slats from warping, I laid them on newspaper on my bench and weighted them down with a plywood sheet and weights until they dried out.

I stripped the drawers next, then the desk top which held the roll, and the wood frame around the leather writing surface. To strip the desk base, I flipped it over and placed the piece on a 14-in. (35-cm) worktable in order to strip it upside down since the critical surfaces were at the bottom and difficult to reach when the desk was right-side up. I removed all the old leather from the writing surface and the panel on which it had been glued and then glued new leather on the panel, using special leather glue. I then weighted it and left it to dry.

The new canvas that was to hold down the rolltop was purchased at an awning supply house, cut to fit and laid out on a large table. Using glue and wood staples, I secured the end of the rolltop that remained in the desk cavity. I poured glue on the canvas, spread it evenly and sparingly, and put the wooden slat in place. I laid plywood on top of the slats and weighted it, and left the canvas to dry.

I was able to replace a missing scroll and foot with my hand-carved ones. The refinishing then began with sanding and the application of a fruit-colored stain. After it dried, I brushed on a sealer of thinned polyurethane, lightly sanded the surfaces after they had dried, wiped everything with a tack cloth, and brushed on the full-strength polyurethane. I cleaned the brass handles and put them back on the drawers. Several days later, I applied a very light sanding to make the furniture surfaces smooth. All this took me about 45 hours to complete.

Secretaries

Secretaries, be they Renaissance or Mission style, have glazed door tops, as well as pull-down writing surfaces. In either case, interiors show, meaning that interiors will probably have to be refinished (which just about doubles your work). The pigeon holes in the desk-writing areas are a particularly difficult part to strip. As they are often just very dirty, try washing them first. You may have to remove them to really be able to soak off the grime. Even if they must be stripped, they are much easier to work out of the desk rather than in; you generally have to work on the interior while bending over the opened writing surface.

Removing shelves from cases whose interiors you plan to strip is the best procedure. Strip them separately. You may also want to remove the writing drop-leaf surface to give you better access to the carcass.

Built-ins

The rooms most likely to have built-ins are the kitchen, dining room and library. In the kitchen, the built-in is usually a cupboard or cabinet, both of which are considered architectural pieces. In the dining room, however, the sideboard is really a piece of furniture. It differs from the latter built-ins in that it sometimes doesn't have sides, back or top. It also differs in construction because it was built by a carpenter and was probably first finished by a house painter. The typical sideboard has probably been refinished more often than the typical antique because it was considered to be a part of the woodwork.

Because the built-in sideboard has more coats of varnish or paint, your refinishing task will be more difficult. Add that to the fact that most sideboards have glazed cabinet doors, meaning that their interiors probably also need restoration, and you have a big job ahead of you. You can save a lot of time by using the electric paint remover if there are two or more coats of paint covering any surface. This tool heats paint to the point where it is plastic enough to scrape off with a stiff putty knife or hooked paint scraper. Caution: The electric paint remover can singe or burn, so be careful. Do not use it in conjunction with chemical paint remover because combustion is likely to occur.

Built-in bookshelves probably still retain their initial finish. If you have a problem with them, you may want to investigate a commercial, spray finish-remover to strip at least the shelves, maybe even a dip strip place that is very dependable. Take a few shelves over to see what the firm can do; if you like the price and the results, have all the shelves done to save you time and energy.

Strange antique pieces I have stripped

Searching through my scrapbook and my memory, I recall refinishing painted washstands, Thonet bentwood chairs, a Sheraton drop-leaf table, Empire chests, Victorian occasional tables, sewing machine cabinets, store counters, mellodion desks, a jeweler's bench, a brass bed, a dental cabinet and much more. All of which goes to prove that anything can be stripped. All you have to do is know what you're doing and what final results to expect; be patient, since stripping will at first take a lot of time.

4   *Finishing Furniture*

A lot of emphasis recently has been put on furniture stripping (and that's often as far as some people get). But stripping is just the mechanical process that gets restoration down to bare wood; it is when you start from scratch that you need all the artistry, skill and creativeness you can muster. It's also when the fun begins, and in the finishing phase you can see the fruit of your efforts.

Objectives

Ideally, the furniture piece should look a lot like it did when it was made. It should possess an appropriate color and an even color coverage. The wood tone should, for example, be a medium to dark walnut for a high Victorian walnut chest, a golden oak for an Eastlake desk, and a darker oak for a Mission Oak hall tree.

The tone should also be relatively even, meaning that there are no visible streaks or brush strokes. Your tabletop should not be lighter at one end than at the other; chest drawer fronts should look like they belong to the carcass which houses them. Repairs, patches and sanding should blend in with the rest of the piece. Of course, color unevenness due to wood grain variations is acceptable because it is natural.

Another finishing objective is smoothness. As we shall see later in this chapter, a smooth surface is achieved by proper wood preparation and finish application.

Your finish should be durable, so finish your tables so they can hold alcoholic drinks and plant pots. Restore your chairs so they can withstand both food spills and back-tilts on the rear legs.

Choosing the Right Color

While you may wish to use a finish color that is faithful to the original finish of an antique, there are certain color ranges to keep in mind. For example, golden oak can wander from a pale yellow, through brownish yellow, and reddish-brown yellow to a light fruitwood, in my opinion. Surely there was no standard industry color for that style in 1900; in fact, there was no label "golden oak" during that

61

period. Just as golden oak is not standardized, neither is maple. Maple comes in pale, red, brown red tones, some almost golden red.

Ask yourself if you are personally attracted to lighter or darker shades. How is the room presently decorated? Looking at your carpeting or rug, drapes and wall coverings, what colors, tones and shades predominate? If you plan to re-decorate, what is the general decor you wish to establish?

Your house style, if classification is possible, may also be an important factor in selecting furniture wood tones. Colonial could call for maple and other Early American or Primitive colors; California Mission, on the other hand, calls for darker wood colors, contrasting with the lighter, bleached shades of an Art Deco motif. The eclectic or "clutter" style permits a grand mixing of tones.

Still another consideration is timelessness versus trendiness. Extreme tones— dark and light—may be trendy; that is, in one year and out the other. Medium tones, I feel, have a more timeless quality to them.

Let's say for the purpose of illustration, that your Renaissance Victorian secre-tary will be a focal point in your room. What should it really look like? It was originally a dark walnut, meaning that you have to stain the walnut wood. On the other hand, perhaps a lighter shade of walnut would be better. Maybe the natural color of the wood is just perfect. How can you really know? Testing should tell you.

There may come a time, however, when that table that you did "natural" will better fit with your decor or be worth much more if it is refinished to its original color, say dark Victorian walnut. You can strip the two or three coats of poly-urethane you brushed on, and start refinishing all over again, only this time begin with a dark walnut stain.

At times, you may have to refinish something over again because of technical problems. For example, I stripped paint from a side chair for a daughter and finished it natural several years ago. I later stripped the table and other side chairs of that suite and discovered to my dismay that the tabletop was so distressed that a natural finish would be a mistake. So, the tabletop and the chair were stained fruitwood. This meant that the first chair I'd stripped had to be stripped, stained and finished to match the suite.

Natural Color vs. Stained Color

By "natural color," I mean the color that the particular antique piece has acquired over time, previous finishes and Mother Nature. The only way to find out the true natural color of wood is to apply a sealer. Since that would interfere with other wood finishes, the next best procedure is to test color by using a solvent

Oak

Maple

such as benzene, paint thinner or turpentine. Wipe some solvent on the wood and note the color before it dries: That is about what your furniture piece would look like refinished "natural."

If you like the natural color, what else has this finish got going for it? Well, there is absolutely no pigment that can cover the grain; therefore, beautiful grains such as walnut can show in all their natural glory. Not having to stain the antique eliminates one finishing step, saving you both time and money.

If you don't like the natural color, you will have to stain the piece. Stain helps achieve more color evenness where this is a problem. Then, too, some stains have a rather heavy pigment, which helps cover up defects. So, if your stripping revealed blemishes you'd rather hide, stain the surfaces with a heavy pigment material.

Stain can also provide a more satisfactory color than the natural wood. Pine and mahogany are two examples of wood that often need help in the color area. Natural pine often can have an insipid appearance; and mahogany, when it is stripped, is often very red, a color accentuated only by sealer application. On the other hand, a medium-to-dark brown color with some green in it produces the lovely dark-brown mahogany that just about everyone likes.

Finish Application Methods

The ways in which you can apply finishing materials are your hands, a cloth, a brush and a spray gun.

Some people consider rubbing tung oil into the wood surface with their hands to be the best approach. It may well be appropriate, though some say it is a slow process. There are others who prefer to wipe stain or stain-sealers into the wood with cloth, and some stains are called "wiping stains." Cloth may give you more control over tone, and it is certainly cheaper and more convenient to use than the average brush. If the tone you have applied is too dark, you can wipe some of it off with the cloth; if staining is too light, it can be darkened by rubbing a little more into the wood. There are, however, several disadvantages to using cloth. One is the danger of rubbing lint into the furniture surface; another is the time-consuming effort the wiping process takes. I achieve tone control by getting the color right in the beginning through proper mixing and testing.

I have always used a brush for finish application, though I used to buy cheaper brushes when I first started refinishing. The brushes I currently use are the best China bristle available, and they are super clean. A China bristle brush is clean and fast and does not give you stained cuticles, though it is expensive and requires care. Brush marks are always a possibility for the beginner, too.

Proper brushing entails a clean, relatively new China bristle brush that's wide enough to do a good fast job. I use widths from 2 to 3 in. (5 to 7.6 cm), the wider brush being used for large surfaces, such as tabletops. The finish stroke should continue in one long sweep, parallel with the wood grain. You should place only light pressure on it. If you brush this way, you should have no finishing marks.

In addition to proper brushing, finishing marks can be avoided by stripping all of the old finish off the surface, sanding well, and properly thinning the stripping material. The road to a hand-rubbed look is a correctly thinned sealer and finish. Conversely, thick material tends to give a finished surface a "painted" look.

Spray application techniques are gaining popularity among professional furniture refinishers for the same reason that all modern furniture makers use them: speed. Lacquer, the finish on many professionally finished antiques (especially those at antique shows), is applied with a spray gun. The advantage of the spray process is that it applies a fast-drying material that doesn't collect dust while in the process of drying. Shop conditions, therefore, don't have to be as clean as when varnish is being brushed on. The disadvantage of lacquer is that it is not the original finish on 99 percent of the antiques, and the principle of faithfulness to the original is violated when lacquer is applied. Lacquer is not as stable a finish as varnish, and it has to be applied with some rather sophisticated equipment and techniques, beyond the scope of the average weekend stripper.

Preparing to Finish

Now that you've selected a color and method of finishing, you can turn to the actual finishing process. Check to see that all of the old finish is gone.

Despite your best efforts, old finish may still be in corners of side panel frames, in incised lines, against applied vines and flowers, or, worst of all, in the surface wood grain. By now this residue is dry and somewhat brittle, making its removal more a matter of patience than of strength. Scrape out what you can; what you can't remove after a decent time interval, forget until the sealing step, when you can touch it up. Be cautious when scraping near applied decorations like vines and flowers since they break and come off quite easily. Getting dried residue—be it varnish or paint—from corners, incisions and carvings should be done with the largest tool you have. So rather than using a hairpin, use a 1-in. (2.5-cm) bevelled chisel or a butcher knife. Sharpened and pointed, these tools can dig and scrape off residue. If old finish remains on flat surfaces, sanding can remove much of it.

Sanding

Sanding consists of surface-material removal by an abrasive called sandpaper. Sandpaper comes in sheets of various grades and several quality levels. I use it in grades 36 to 220 and use wet and dry sandpaper in grades 320, 400 and 600. Just in case you're not familiar with grade numbers, the lower the number, the coarser the grade and the more material that can be removed at a given time. Many people seem afraid to use very coarse paper, and they subject themselves to a lot more work; however, use the coarse grades when you have a lot of sanding to do.

WHEN TO USE SANDPAPER. The time to use sandpaper when restoring furniture is just after the piece has been stripped. The stripping process raises wood grain which must be made smooth again.

WHEN NOT TO USE SANDPAPER. Sandpaper is a very poor finish remover because it does not penetrate enough surface so as to get at sealers and pigments. It is also a poor tool for removing too much remaining residue from the stripping step. Too much remaining residue indicates a poor stripping job; get out the stripper and have a go at it again because stripper is much faster and more effective than sandpaper.

OVERSANDING. Since sanding not only removes wood, but may inordinately lighten the wood or a portion of a wood surface, use caution. Since tabletops often need more sanding than the legs, and are certainly much more accessible, I frequently run across the work of others in which the top refinishes two shades lighter than the legs. This is one result of oversanding, I believe; if you have committed such an error, merely darken the stain used for the top of the piece and stain the remainder the normal shade.

Oversanding is a common problem, but you may wonder how to determine you've sanded enough. Use both tactile and visual examination to answer that question. Does it *feel* smooth, and when looking at the surface into a light, does it *look* smooth? Is there an even tonal appearance? Is the surface dull? If the answers to these questions are yes, then you're through sanding. Most antiques are expected to be somewhat more rough than furniture in a modern showroom display.

HOW TO USE SANDPAPER. Sandpaper should be used in such a way that it does not scratch, gouge or "dish" the surface. Sand *with* the grain (there are exceptions), sand lightly, sand with a flat surface, and sand evenly.

For large surface areas, I fold a large sheet of sandpaper in quarters to give solid and extensive coverage. For smaller areas, I use a quarter piece folded in half. One should always sand with the coarsest grade sandpaper possible and quickly move to less coarse grades. I frequently start with number 80 grit, then sand with number 120 and wind up with number 180. The sheet or folded areas of sandpaper should be turned frequently; wood dust that clog the paper should be quickly removed by rubbing another sheet of sandpaper on your worksheet.

HAND-SANDING VS. MACHINE-SANDING. Perhaps you've noted that up to this point

I've been writing about hand-sanding. The reason is that I do not own a mechanical sander because I've learned to reduce the need for sanding to a minimum through correct stripping, and I've learned how to hand-sand so as to minimize time and effort. As noted, many antiques do not have the finish that store-bought lacquered pieces have.

Finally, I don't have a machine sander because I'm afraid of oversanding. So, before you belt- or disc-sand anything, ask yourself whether you'll be able to duplicate this finish and this wood color with machine-sanding over the entire surface of this piece. For most antiques, the answer will be "no." This is because there are panels, curves, applied decorations, mouldings and surface areas adjacent to them that will have to be hand-sanded due to the machine's inability to reach them.

Machine-sanding certainly has its place. In refinishing floors, shelves and flush doors, this mode definitely saves you time and effort. I suggest, however, that you limit the machine to such surfaces as those mentioned and do not use it on antique furniture.

Sandpaper should be folded into quarters to provide even pressure.

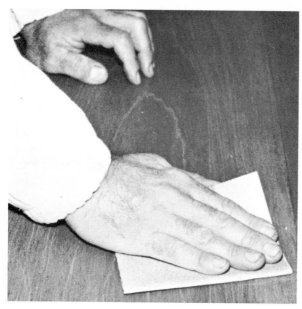

Sand with the grain in even-pressured, long strokes.

Begin sanding with a coarse grade, here a number 80, and end with a fine grade, such as number 180. Note how clean the wood surface looks after final sanding, compared to the nonsanded surface in the foreground.

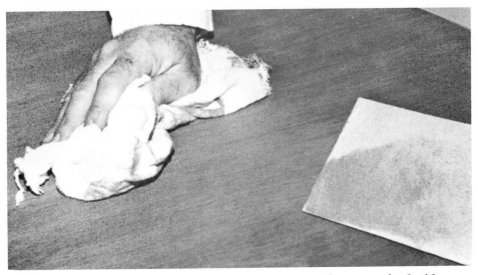

Since this particular sanding created a lot of dust, the surface was wiped with a rag and then a tack cloth.

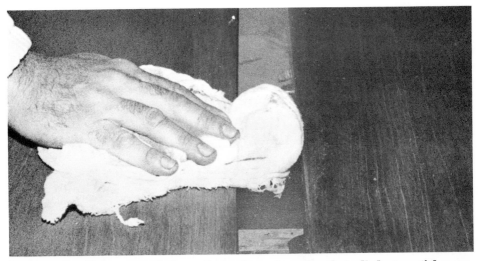

Surfaces should be separated, as shown here, in order that all dust particles are removed from the furniture.

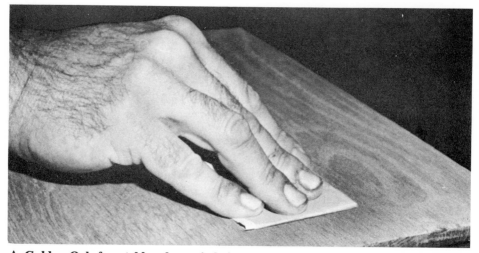

A Golden Oak fern table, above, is being sanded with 80 grade production sandpaper, to be followed by a sanding with 120 grade and 180 grade sandpaper.

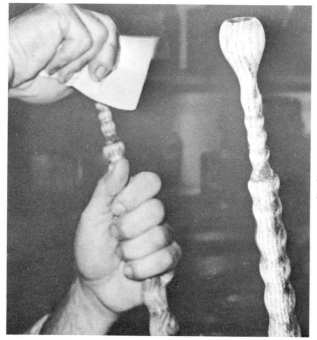

Small pieces of furniture should be flipped over so that feet and undersides are more accessible. Sanding turned legs involves vertical sanding with the grain and sanding in the turnings.

A tack cloth is being used to mop up sanding dust.

Staining Techniques

In this section we're going to look at the different kinds of stains, their color variations and the different coverages you can expect.

KINDS OF STAIN. Wood stains are manufactured today as penetrating oil stains, water stains, spirit (alcohol) stains, and pigment oil stains. Of these, penetrating oil stains are the most common and what I recommend. They are made by dissolving coal-tar dyes in naphtha, benzene or turpentine. Available in a variety of colors, they also come in forms for wiping on and brushing on. Though some stains are specifically labelled "wiping," brushing stains can also be wiped on, or off; I, however, prefer to brush on all materials.

The advantage of penetrating oil stains is that they are premixed and ready to use. They are also easy to apply and do the job for which they are intended. One is cautioned in their use, since paste fillers and varnishes applied directly over them tend to soften them, and polyurethane sealers may cause the stain to bleed.

While some refinishers seal oil stain with shellac to prevent such bleeding, I have found that allowing the stain to dry for one to three days, depending upon the amount of humidity present, results in a very satisfactory surface seal. Working the brush back and forth unnecessarily while applying the sealer will reactivate the stain because it has the same solvent as varnish and polyurethane.

The colors available in oil stains, some feel, are rather limited for professional work. I disagree. One prominent manufacturer offers 11 different colors, and another has 16. A good paint store can mix 14 additional colors for you, and you will learn in this chapter how to mix your own stain colors.

The advantages of water stains achieved by dissolving aniline dyes in water are: more shades, nonfading, and nonmixing with sealers and finish coats. Their principal disadvantage for restoration is that they will not penetrate surfaces from which the finish has been previously removed. Also, they take a lot of time and trouble to mix.

Spirit stains are produced by dissolving alcohol-soluble powders in alcohol, and, because they are fast-drying, they are great for touch-up and staining small objects. So that leaves us with penetrating oil stains for antique furniture restoration, with all its advantages and disadvantages.

Color varieties

Working with colors in antique furniture refinishing is a skill which one achieves with experience. As noted earlier, stain manufacturers produce certain standard colors. Some even have the same name, such as fruitwood and maple. However, the fruitwood of one brand is not the identical color of a fruitwood of another brand. So once you start with one brand, finish with it. The color you get in restoring an antique piece depends on the wood variety, surface preparation, the number of coats of stain applied, and whether or not you wipe the stained surface after brushing on the stain.

All these variables make it necessary for you to test the stain before you begin the job. Do this by putting a little stain on your finger and daubing it on the restoration piece in an unobtrusive spot. Wipe that off with a little solvent after you're through testing. If you don't like the color when you're completely through staining, simply wipe off as much as you can with a rag soaked in a mineral spirit solvent and strip the piece with paint-and-varnish remover. Hint: In order to start staining immediately, use a mineral spirit solvent instead of water in the wash phase of the stripping process. Let that dry a short time, and you can restain.

Covering differences

The coverage qualities of different brands differ, too. This does not necessarily make one better than another; it gives you a choice. If the piece you're restoring has a perfectly clear wood surface, a beautiful grain and the stripping job was superior, you may want to choose a brand with less covering power. If, on the other hand, stripping reveals surface defects that sanding could not remove, get a stain that will cover those defects.

Mixing stains

When I first started in this business I stained antiques any color customers wanted as long as it was fruitwood. I later discovered that there were other suitable stain colors, but I still used the shades offered by stain makers straight from the can. It wasn't until some customers requested colors that required mixing that I began to mix stains. And, to my surprise, I found that with some practice, the results are excellent!

HOW TO MIX. You can mix the stains of the *same* manufacturer. Here are a few parameters for mixing: To get red, use mahogany; to lighten the mix, use platinum; to achieve brown, I use English oak; and to darken, I use Flemish black. In actual mixing, first mix very small quantities, keeping track of the number of spoonfuls of each color used. Test the mixture on the wood you intend to refinish. If tests prove satisfactory, be sure to mix enough to complete the whole job.

THINNING STAIN. Just as oil stains can be mixed, they can also be thinned. The purpose of thinning is to lighten the shade. It is the same color, but it is a little lighter after thinning. In some respects, you can get the same results with wiping the stain after application, but in thinning you eliminate the potential lint deposits of the wiping process. To thin, just mix mineral spirit solvents with the stain to the desired viscosity.

How to stain

Stain should be brushed on the antique piece because this method permits more coverage. Your brush should be very clean; that is, free of lint and dirt. If it's a new brush, wipe it with a tack cloth before using it to eliminate any factory or store dust. Good China bristle brushes are much better for fine refinishing than synthetic bristles.

Dirt is the enemy of good refinishing. Furniture surfaces should be free of sanding dust, lint and other dirt. Clean surfaces to be stained with a tack cloth and clean interiors of pieces with a vacuum cleaner. Chairs and other pieces whose feet directly touch the floor should be dusted and set on clean newspaper so that the brush doesn't pick up any floor dirt.

Try to work in a clean area. Whether you work in a basement, garage or barn, the floor should be swept clean, and open doors and windows should not allow dust in.

Brush stain completely across large horizontal surfaces, such as tabletops, before you leave them to dry, thus eliminating brush-stroke ends. This will cause drips on edges, which you can correct with a brush or rag. In staining vertical sections, start below the top with a brushful of stain, and brush down a little before you brush up. This helps prevent runs. Poke plenty of stain in corners, and check for missed spots. In general, stain need not be applied generously, so brush it out until the brush is practically dry.

Sometimes stain runs and drips. One way to avoid this is to keep your brush relatively dry. Even then a drip will occur, so keep an eye open for it. Before you quit for the day, check the piece for drips. Any that you note can usually be corrected with wiping, taking care not to unduly lighten the area. If you miss a run, take a cloth with a little mineral spirits on it and carefully wipe the drip. That should take care of it.

Other color finishes

Several other color finishes deserve mention, although they combine stain with other ingredients. One is a sealer-stain, and the other a varnish-stain. The sealer-stain combines sealer and stain, and is supposed to eliminate the sealing step in the finishing process. While it may well do that, my experience with one brand of this substance indicates that two more coats must be put on over it to give a satisfactory finish. Nonetheless, there are two advantages to its use. One is that bleeding

Stain should be brushed on with even strokes.

seems to be eliminated, probably because the stain is stabilized in the wood surface. The other advantage is the clear finish that sealer-stain provides. However, it does cost more than ordinary penetrating oil stain.

Varnish-stain is a combination of varnish and stain and is designed to be used when very serious refinishing problems are present; thus, it is a good cover-up for a poorly stripped piece. This cover-up also hides wood grain, and the thick viscosity of varnish-stain makes both brushing difficult and brush marks more likely, in my opinion. It seems to have very limited usage in the restoration of antique furniture.

Sealing Antique Furniture

Sealing means protecting the stained surface, as well as the unstained, from the elements. In the "natural" finish process, it's the first step in refinishing; when staining, it's the second. It is undoubtedly the easiest task in restoration.

Material alternatives

There are also alternatives to sealing, including shellac, natural varnish, synthetic varnish (polyurethane), sealer-stains and tung oil.

SHELLAC. This material has been the all-time favorite. Throughout the centuries it has been the mainstay of the wood refinisher because it's fast-drying, protects relatively well, and is relatively long-lasting. There are many museum pieces finished with shellac. However, shellac is generally unsatisfactory, since it's not waterproof or heatproof.

Shellac turns white when exposed to moisture, and it darkens wood with age. A hot dish placed on a shellacked surface will soften it and mark it. Where liquor is apt to be present on a shellacked surface, the shellac is in danger because alcohol is the solvent of shellac. In my experience, since shellac sets up (dries) rather quickly, brush marks are a distinct possibility.

Shellac will not react with oil stains, as noted, and dries quickly, an advantage in humid climates and where serious dust conditions exist. If you choose shellac as a sealer, you must thin it to a 2.5-lb. (1.2-L) cut with denatured alcohol; for example, to the typical paint-store-variety quart (.9 L) of 3-lb. (1.4-kg) cut, you need to add about half a pint (.2 L) of denatured alcohol. Since shellac also dries quickly in its container, thin it a little more as you work if you are doing a lot of shellacking.

NATURAL VARNISH. You may also use thinned natural varnish to seal *if* you intend to finish-coat the piece with this material. Although varnish is generally thought of as a finish coat, manufacturers give directions on the can for its application as a sealer. Although I have rarely used natural varnish for sealing, I now use synthetic varnish exclusively as a sealer (and with great success).

COMMERCIAL SEALERS. A few commercial sealers on the market can be used if natural varnish is to be the finish coat. In my opinion they are unnecessary, duplicating either shellac, thinned natural varnish, or thinned polyurethane.

POLYURETHANE. Polyurethane is a synthetic varnish or "finish" (as I prefer to call it), available from a number of manufacturers, sometimes under different names. In its thinned state, it is a very suitable sealer. The principal advantage is that two coats of polyurethane, the sealer and the finish coat, give the antique a very tough surface, resistant to practically everything. As a sealer, it effectively seals out moisture and dryness.

The principal disadvantage of polyurethane as a sealer is that it uses the same mineral spirit solvent as oil stain and may cause bleeding (amalgamation or muddying-up of the stain). Bleeding can be controlled, as noted, by allowing the oil stain time enough to dry, and by proper brush application of the sealer. Of course, in natural finishing, this is no problem. Another fault of polyurethane cited by some people is that its use on furniture surfaces results in a plastic look. I have never had this problem. Perhaps the reasons are the brand of polyurethane I use, the fact that I thin it by mixing about one-quarter thinner to three-quarters polyurethane, and I give the piece an appropriate sanding both after sealing and after the finish coat.

TUNG OIL. Tung oil is a varnish derived from the tung nut, an ingredient of varnish for years. Most producers combine it with other ingredients such as thinners and dryers. Though it is being used by weekend refinishers with increasing popularity, most of the old masters in refinishing I have consulted make no mention of it. Tung oil is somewhat controversial; its proponents speak very highly of it, saying it allows wood to breathe and gives furniture a hand-rubbed look. That may well be; however, if wood breathes, it must take in humidity and/or dryness. Users of tung oil have told me that it's slow-drying and usually requires several coats to look good. If you decide to use this material, do not apply it over varnished, lacquered, shellacked or synthetically finished surfaces.

Sealing techniques

When stripping, your goal was the removal of all old finish, and in staining, it was even coverage. Here all you have to do is just brush on the sealer, and an occasional run or drip can be scraped off with a fingernail once the sealer dries.

If the natural finish (no stain) process is being followed, be certain all dust is gone by using a tack cloth on surfaces and a vacuum for corners and interiors. It is also important to dust the undersides of pieces because refinishing dust can fall on such components as chair stretchers and table legs. Even if you cleaned for staining, wipe the surfaces again for possible lint, dust and cat hairs that might have accumulated overnight.

Again, use a super clean brush and avoid brush marks. Watch for drips and runs under chair stretchers and under table edges. While even coverage is desirable, it is not absolutely necessary. What gets lighter treatment in this step can be corrected in the finish step. High humidity may lengthen the drying time of the sealer if it's spread over stain.

The Finish Coat

In preparation for the final step in refinishing antique furniture, one must lightly sand the sealed surfaces, touch up surface defects, and fill any holes.

SANDING. Sanding the sealed surfaces, in contrast to sanding before staining or sealing if you're finishing the piece natural, is a much lighter task. All you want to accomplish is smoothing the grain that's been raised by the sealer. Often there is very little roughness; there is always some, though.

When I started in this field, steel wool was the recommended material for smoothing fibres raised by sealing. While it is still useful for fine carvings and turnings, its use is severely limited because of the bits of broken steel and fuzz it leaves (especially in hard-to-get-at places). Consequently, use wet and dry sandpaper, used dry.

Wet and dry sandpaper is the same material auto refinishers use to make car finishes so smooth. I suggest that you use either grade 400 or 600, depending on the extent of grain-raising, grade 400 being more coarse. For turnings, mouldings, edges and carvings, use worn number 600 because it is less likely to scratch.

Sand lightly with the grain wherever possible, and wipe the piece with a tack cloth afterward. Sanding generally gives the wood a duller, whitish look; the color will return to its sealed color when you apply the finish coat.

TOUCH-UP. I usually wait until the true color of the piece is revealed after the sealing before doing minor touch-ups. The sealer prevents any area not to be touched up from acquiring additional color. Excess touch-up can easily be wiped from surface areas adjacent to the defect. More information on how to touch up furniture is covered in Chapter 6.

FILLING. As with touch-up, filling is also done at this stage of restoration, and for exactly the same reasons. Filling works better in corners than in the middle of a highly polished dining table. Therefore, it may be best at times to let the defect be. For more information on filling, see Chapter 6.

Materials

The materials needed for the finish coat are the same as those noted in the sealing and staining phases of restoration. Following are some general comments to guide you.

Natural varnish has a warmth and softness which is unexcelled, I think. Its flowing and levelling tendencies are also excellent, but for most modern living it does not protect furniture surfaces as well as synthetic varnish.

With the exception of warmth, depth and softness, polyurethane has all the qualities of natural varnish, plus one more: It's definitely tougher. Polyurethane tends to produce a flatter appearance, resembling hand-rubbed surfaces, if handled correctly. Thin it if your container has been previously opened or if you have been doing a lot of finishing.

Lacquer has the advantage of fast application with a spray gun—do not brush it on—and is equally fast-drying. It is also somewhat heat-and-moisture resistant and will not oxidize or change into powder with age. Lacquer is, however, subject to blushing and requires some skill to avoid problems such as dry spray peeling and pinhole-rough surfaces. Also, this material cannot be applied over varnish or painted surfaces, and oil-stained surfaces must be shellacked first.

Finish techniques

Good lighting is a must; I like to use a strong sidelight on the antique piece while brushing on the finish coat. The finish coat has a wet look for a while, and missed spots show up since unfinished surfaces look dull and do not reflect any light. Wetness is also beneficial in spotting drips and runs because after everything has dried, runs still look wet.

It's also helpful to know where runs typically occur. Such places are where stretchers and seat rails join chair legs, where tops of tables and desks meet legs, on all side panels, and on spool-turned members. Avoid runs on drawer fronts by removing them and finishing them on a horizontal plane. Drop-leaf table-drop sections should be left to dry in as horizontal a position as possible while permitting the joining edges enough air and space to dry properly. Finally, check again for drips.

Another finish coat

At times your antique restoration may need a second finish coat, although it is generally good to avoid it because too great a material buildup results and the "natural" look is gone. The indication that a second finish coat is necessary is a dull, absorbed-finish look to the job. In other words, it looks like the finish coat was all soaked up by the wood. Furniture that has for years been subjected to very dry conditions will often be seeking a finish when stripped. Also, natural finish jobs, not having the benefit of oil stain to feed the wood, require another finish coat.

If applying a second finish coat, sand the first finish coat more than ordinarily recommended, and use the tack cloth. To avoid a heavily varnished look, thin the mixture (though not as much as the sealer coat).

Final sanding

After leaving the piece to dry a few days to be certain the finish coat is *really* set and hard, take a piece of very worn number 600 wet and dry sandpaper and, using it dry, very lightly sand all surfaces. I like to call this "dusting," because that's as little pressure as you should put on it.

The reason for this final sanding is to clear the surfaces of small lint and dust particles that managed to get there despite your care. In the old days they used pumice for this task; today we have wet and dry sandpaper. Just be careful not to remove any sheen; you can't correct missed gouges now, nor can you take care of brush marks. It's too late for that, so be content to just remove the hardened fuzzles. Sanding under strong light will tell you whether you are destroying any sheen. Sometimes a hardened piece of lint or a broken paintbrush hair that's embedded in the finish coat can be carefully removed with a fingernail.

Light sanding with number 600 wet/dry sandpaper used dry takes off any slight residue caused by a slightly raised grain. Wipe surface with a tack cloth after sanding.

A new oak base was custom-made for this table, now restored. While the top and base grains do not match, the finishes do.

Manufactured about 1890, this fern table is now in its refinished state.

Frank Lloyd Wright Furniture

The Frank Lloyd Wright dining suite owned by the Frank Lloyd Wright Home and Studio Foundation, and that owned by the Unity Temple Restoration Foundation, had to be refinished according to certain requirements. Both had color objectives, and both had to be able to stand up to tour groups and special events like concerts.

In the case of Wright's former home, the furniture had to be restored to its original color. Since no records were kept pertaining to the color of Wright's furniture, a lot of time was spent discussing the color. A restoration committee member hit upon the idea that since the furniture was originally in the 1889 dining room, and the built-in cabinet was still in place, maybe the clue lay there. A search discovered that the original color was still on the inside of the cabinet doors, albeit covered with dirt and several coats of shellac and varnish.

I very lightly stripped the cabinet door backs, uncovering the original reddish-golden oak, typical of the late Victorian era. Then I sealed and varnished them to bring out the finished color. That has become the color standard for all the woodwork restoration in that edifice, and that of the dining suite.

The Frank Lloyd Wright table shown here has been stripped and sanded.

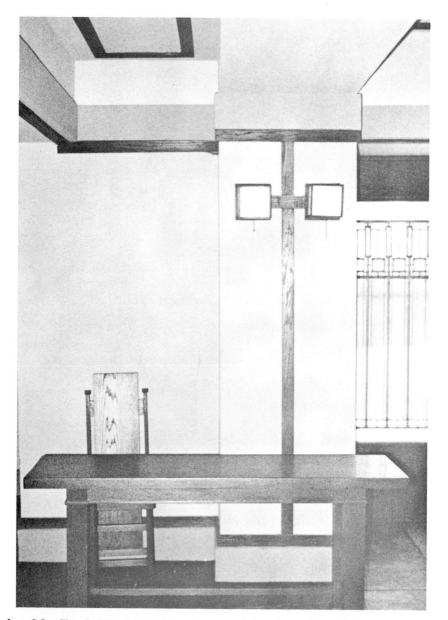

Designed by Frank Lloyd Wright and restored by the author, this table and chair can be found in the Frank Lloyd Wright Unity Temple in Oak Park, Illinois. Note how the chair back matches the woodwork.

Also restored by the author, this Wright chair is part of the Wright Unity Temple collection.

The next task was to match that color so that the furniture, when finished, was also of that color. Just staining the furniture was not enough: We had to know what the wood looked like with both stain and sealer. The stain mix consists of three shades of a national manufacturer's brand.

The furniture was both sealed and finished with polyurethane to add a very durable seal since the furniture is sometimes used by the public. The dining room has been used for numerous committee meetings and other events since the restoration was completed in December 1977.

At Unity Temple, research had been conducted that identified the original color of the woodwork. As the furniture restorer, I was asked to match that color as well as I could.

Here, surprisingly, the natural color of the high-backed chairs and tables, when stripped and sealed, was an exact match. The slant-backed chairs, a Flemish-black color because of repeated coats of varnish stain over the years, came out a little darker than the woodwork when stripped and sealed. All the Wright-designed furniture I restored at Unity Temple was sealed and finished with polyurethane because of the heavy traffic and the pieces now look as if they belong together.

5   *Caning and Reupholstering*

This chapter comes after furniture repairing, stripping and refinishing because that is the recommended order in the restoration process. The time to repair a chair is *before* it has been caned, not when you're finished. If you plan to cane a chair and not refinish it, give it the old defect test: Put your knee on the seat or seat frame, grasp the back and try to rock it. If it moves, it needs repair.

If you have ever had to refinish a chair with an upholstered fabric bottom that was to survive the process unscathed, you will definitely want to strip and refinish first. Though there is a danger of damaging the chair's finish in the upholstering or caning process, damage to the upholstery is much less likely to occur than if you strip and refinish the chair first.

Chair Caning

Chair caning consists of either the seven-step hand-woven bottom, or the much easier sheet-cane installation.

What are caned chair bottoms?

Antique chairs that were originally caned come into your possession in one of four conditions. The chair has no bottom at all; it has a hand-caned bottom and is probably an older chair; it has a sheet-caned bottom (the caning is manufactured and put in place in one sheet); or it may have what I call a "covered" cane bottom. (The opening for the cane was cut by the chair-maker and the grooves for the sheet cane spline is in place.) If it is an older chair, holes for handwoven cane have been drilled.

I have seen all kinds of covers on cane chairs, including carpeting, plywood and composite board. Sometimes all the old cane was removed, but the old spline is left inside. To determine whether or not your piece was hand-caned, turn it over and see if cane holes are present. For sheet-cane identification, you'll have to remove the cover to see if a router groove has been cut.

In the event your chair was not originally caned by its manufacturer, you can still cane it, though the chair will no longer be faithful to the original. If you want to handweave a cane bottom, drill ³⁄₁₆-in. (4.7-mm) holes with centers spaced ½ in. (1.2 cm) apart, and drilled about ½ in. (1.2 cm) inside the inside edge of the chair seat frame. I suggest that an even number of holes be drilled and that the underneath end of each hole be slightly countersunk to facilitate weaving.

The spline groove, cut either with a router or by hand with a universal plane and chisel, should measure a standard ¼-in. (6-mm) depth and a ³⁄₁₆-in. (4.7-mm) width. It should lie about an inch (2.5 cm) inside the inside edge of the chair seat frame and can have either square corners or rounded ones.

What is chair cane?

Cane is a term that's applied to a great number of plants having long, slender, reedlike stems, although it originally came from a class of palms. Today cane comes from the outer bark of stems that are 100 ft. to 300 ft. (30 m to 91 m) in length and 1 in. (2.5 cm) in diameter. The outer bark is stripped into widths varying from ¹⁄₁₆ in. (1.6 mm) to ³⁄₁₆ in. (4.7 mm), about 10 ft. (3 m) long and bundled into a hank of 1,000 lineal feet for handweaving purposes. Cane can be purchased by the hank from upholstery supply house and craftsmen's suppliers.

Machine-woven cane comes in widths ranging from 8 in. (20 cm) to 18 in. (45 cm) and in rolls of varying lengths. Check the catalogue of your nearest supplier for the widths in which they sell this material, as well as for the patterns they handle. Different mesh sizes are also available, ranging from fine to medium.

TOOLS. Tools used in caning are really very simple and inexpensive, making up for the high cost of the cane. I use an ice pick, scissors, razor blade and wooden pegs such as golf tees for handweaving. For sheet caning, a much simpler and faster process than hand-caning, the required tools are a mallet, a chisel, several hardwood wedges, a spline remover and a razor blade.

How to handweave

Handweaving is often called the seven-step process. Each step can be taken one day at a time and in a week you'll have a new chair bottom.

Before you can start, there are several preparation tasks. Most hand-caned chairs, in my experience, still have some of the old cane left in them. You must, therefore, begin by pulling out the old ratty stuff. Cut it out and pull it from underneath. Typically, the area where the cane covers the chair seat frame is dirty, so it's best to wash it off.

If you intend to refinish the chair, strip and refinish it before caning. Occasionally the chair also needs repair. You must do that first. A serious defect common in hand-caned chairs is that part of the frame splits away from the other part along the line formed by the cane holes. If this is not apparent on your chair, check for it, because if this weakness does exist and is not corrected, subsequent caning will provide the force necessary to pull it apart. About all you can do then to repair it is to cut out all your caning, make the repair, and cane all over again.

Now we are ready for the seven steps. You are facing the back of the chair, the front is the part nearest you, and the two sides are at your right hand and at your left hand. If the chair frame detaches easily, remove it and weave, holding it in your lap. Also, if your chair has arms and they can be removed easily, take them off to simplify your weaving task.

The seven steps are:

1. Side-to-side pull-through

2. Front-to-back pull-through

3. Side-to-side overlay

4. Front-to-back overlay

5. Lower-left to upper-right diagonal weaving

6. Lower-right to upper-left diagonal weaving

7. Binder installation

• *Step One.* After soaking enough strands in warm water and glycerine for one sitting, take the end of one strand and trim it diagonally with scissors. Insert it from above in the upper left-hand hole, one hole from the corner hole. Put a peg in that hole to hold the cane, making sure that enough cane extends through the hole to later tie a knot with it. Carry the cane strand across to the opposite hole, insert it from the top, pull through, and insert it in the bottom of the next hole closer to you. Pull through and carry it to the opposite side, repeating the process. Exert normal, but not undue pulling; also, you may use a peg to hold the cane in a hole before carrying it to the other side of the seat frame. When the cane is pulled completely through that hole, remove the peg from the previous hole, and insert it in the newly completed pull-through. Repeat this process until all holes, except the corner ones, have cane in them. Put a peg in the last hole and leave it there.

• *Step Two.* Starting in the hole next to the corner one in your upper left-hand corner, insert the soaked cane from above and hold it with a peg, allowing enough cane below for later tying. Carry the cane strand over the side-to-side layer and parallel to the seat frame to the hole in the frame closest to you, and insert it through the top and pull it up and through the hole next to it. Put a peg in that hole, and carry the strand to the opposite hole, insert from the top, pull through and over to the next hole, inserting it from underneath. Pull through and up, remove the last holding peg and put it in that hole, and carry the strand to the opposite hole, etc. Repeat this until all holes have been filled except the corner ones. Remember: All pull-throughs and all overlays entail carrying the cane from the *top* of one hole to the *top* of the hole on the opposite frame. Cane goes between adjacent holes from underneath the seat frame. Now, hold the cane in the last hole with a peg.

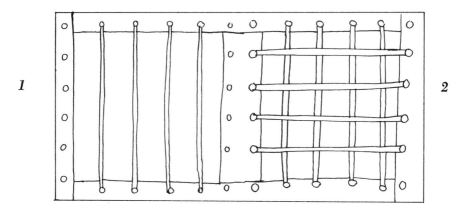

One: Side-to-side pull-through of cane. Two: Front-to-back pull-through of cane.

• *Step Three.* Repeat Step One. Remove the holding peg, insert 4 in. (9 cm) of the soaked strand of cane from the top, and replace the holding peg. Overlay previous cane (Step One) with this new side-to-side layer, carrying it parallel to the front and back sides of the chair-bottom frame until you reach the bottom and hold it in the last hole next to the corner hole in the chair frame. No corner holes should be used.

• *Step Four.* Repeat Step Two. Remove the holding peg in the hole next to the corner hole in the upper left-hand corner. Insert 4 in. (10.2 cm) of soaked cane, leaving enough to tie a knot later, and replace the peg. Carry the cane to the opposite member as you did in Step Two, and repeat the process, overlaying *all* cane already in place.

After completing these four steps, you have two rows of vertical cane and two rows of horizontal cane that are arranged in tictactoe fashion. Only the four corner holes remain unfilled. Pegs still hold both the start and the finish of the four side-to-side pullings and overlays. The reason for not tying yet is that tying covers the holes, and you're not through yet!

• *Step Five.* If the cane that's been laid down is dry, moisten it with cloth. Arrange the strands in pairs, forcing them close together with pegs if necessary. This makes the holes as wide as possible, thus permitting easier subsequent weaving.

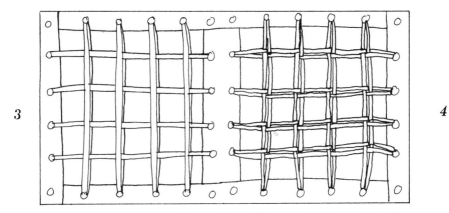

3 **4**

Three: Side-to-side overlay of cane. Four: Front-to-back overlay of cane.

Weave by starting in the lower left-hand corner hole and insert about 4 in. (10.2 cm) of a soaked cane strand. Hold it with a peg. Take the other end of the strand, this time working with a 5-ft. (1.5-m) piece rather than a full length. Carry the end *under* the horizontal (side-to-side) pair of strands, and *over* the vertical (top-to-bottom) pair of strands. Pull to tighten every few holes, but do not pull too hard. When you get to the opposite corner hole, you should have a straight line. Insert the strand end into the hole from the top, pull through and weave either the bottom half of the seat bottom or the top. Complete the process, going *over* the side-to-side pairs, and *under* the top-to-bottom. Put a holding peg in the hole after pulling through 4 in. (9 cm) for tying later on.

If the seat opening is not a perfect square, hold the diagonal cane strand over the cane already in place to first judge where you should go to reach the opposite corner with a relatively straight line. If the opening is definitely a rectangle, you cannot go from corner to corner without getting a weird design, so settle on a point of the corner you wish to connect to. Also, keep the area in which you're weaving wet and slippery with the water-and-glycerine solution.

• *Step Six.* Moisten the cane already in place and repeat Step Five, this time carrying the cane from the lower right-hand corner hole to the upper left-hand corner hole, weaving as you go. Go *over* the side-to-side pairs, and *under* the top-to-bottom.

By now, however, things are getting rather crowded. Holes now have six strands of cane in them, both on the seat and in the frame, so pulling gets more difficult. Keeping just *normal* tension on the cane strands will result in a very tight seat.

• *Step Seven.* In this step you install the binder. Binder cane is by nature wider, and it is designed to cover the holes in the seat frame. Soak it and lay it over the holes, starting in the middle of the back of the seat frame. It is held in place by

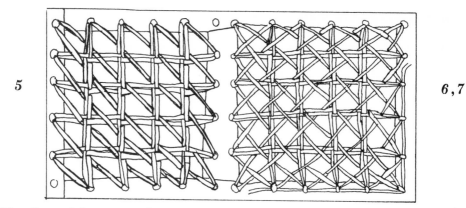

5   6,7

Five: Lower-left to upper-right corner diagonal weaving. Six and Seven: Lower-right to upper-left corner diagonal weaving.

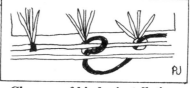

Close-up of binder installation.

very fine cane which is pulled up from underneath, through the seat frame hole, over the binder, and then down through the *same* hole. Carry this "holding" cane underneath the frame to the next hole, push up, go over the binder cane, and push down and pull through. Travel around from the center back, going left, then down one side, across the front, up the other side, and across the back to the center. Since each hole is really crowded, use the ice pick to make a path by pushing cane around.

Now the binder is in place; the design you have made is called the standard weave. The five-step caning standard weave eliminates the pairs of side-to-side and top-to-bottom strands. It does not have the strength of the seven-step standard, the rotary weave and the spider web weave.

Once the binder is in place, you should tie all ends. Since the ends have dried out, use your fingers to moisten them with water and glycerine. Tying consists of wrapping the strand end around any convenient pull-through between holes under the chair-seat frame a few times, then going back through the last wrap and pulling tight. One knot should do it. Cut off remaining material.

Your first chair bottom will take 15 to 20 hours to complete, if it is of average size. In contrast, a professional caner will take about a third of that time and may charge by the hole for the job.

Sheet caning a chair bottom

Simpler installation with the same appearance and, at times, better results are the advantages of commercial, prewoven cane bottoms. Their disadvantage lies in the removal of old cane, the spline that holds it, and the possibility of a caning job that looks lumpy or buckled.

REMOVAL OF OLD CANE AND SPLINE. Your first task is to remove the old caned bottom. While typically all vestiges of the former cane have disappeared, the former spline remains. If it was properly installed, old spline can be dug out without damaging the seat frame.

Start at the seat back where the two ends of the spline meet, and place a very sharp knife point between the spline and its groove on the inside frame side of the groove. Such placement of the tool ensures that any splinters resulting from the spline removal will be covered later by the new cane bottom. Get one end loose and raised so that you can take it in your hand. As you pull up on it, place your scratch awl, ice pick or spline remover under the spline in the groove length-wise and pull up on the tool, exerting a forward push. Try not to break the spline, so you don't have to dig it out again.

Where the spline has been heavily glued in place, you may have to soak it off. I will only do this when the chair is to be stripped and refinished, because soaking in hot water can ruin the finish. The chair seat should be removed for a good soaking in the tub; however, you can try to soak the spline loose by keeping it wet with a Turkish towel. Too much soaking will warp the seat frame. If the seat was removed from the chair, place it under weights while it dries out, and then reassemble the chair. Make all necessary repairs and refinish the piece.

PREPARATION. Measure the caning opening and cut a piece of cane at least an inch (2.5 cm) wider all round the opening. Take the spline and measure the exact length by placing it in the groove. Soak both the piece of sheet cane and the spline in warm water for ten minutes.

CANING. Put synthetic glue into the groove, lay the wet sheet cane over the opening, and line it up carefully so that the side-to-side strands are parallel to the seat-frame front.

With a wooden mallet, pound a hardwood wedge and the cane sheet into the front groove in its center. Leave the wedge in place. Do the same with another wedge in the back groove, pulling the sheet taut; with the other two wedges, do the same for each side. Finally, take a fifth wedge and tap the remaining cane into the grooves, taking care to prevent the sheet from buckling. You should now have the cane bottom tucked into its groove all round the seat frame.

Remove the wedges and pour synthetic glue into the groove again, only this time over the cane. Starting at the center back of the seat frame, tap the spline into place, using a piece of soft wood so as not to put tool marks on the soft spline. If your groove corners are rounded, keep the spline in one piece and follow the curves. If they are square, cut the spline into four pieces, and for a really neat job, cut them at 45° angles so that they meet in the center of the corner.

At times the spline does not want to stay in place after you've tried to tap it. Merely hold it with one or more C-clamps, having first placed a small piece of waxed paper over the clamping spot, then a caul, and then the clamp. Avoid unduly clamping the splines so that they set way below the level of the chair frame.

The final step is cleaning and trimming. Wash off all excess glue, and while the cane is still wet and easy to cut, trim it with a razor blade. Cane should not protrude from under the spline at its outside edge; if it does, sand it after everything is thoroughly dried.

REFINISHING CANE. Cane that's left natural is a very pleasing color that complements nearly all furniture colors, but you can finish handwoven and sheet cane if you wish. Once dried, it can take and hold penetrating oil stains and can be painted. Refinish only the top, seal it and apply polyurethane. Cane left natural should be sealed and finished to ease cleaning and prevent discoloration.

Upholstering Chair Bottoms

Upholstering an antique chair bottom is really an easy task and will certainly improve the appearance of the piece. This activity, however, can get quite complicated when one attempts to redo an entire piece, such as a medallion settee, so, we'll stick to bottoms.

Before we rush into the job, however, here are some things you should consider. You can do as well as the pro when it comes to restoring chair bottoms; it's just that it's going to take you longer! Since there are too many possible upholstering varieties to cover in this chapter, be sure to carefully observe how your particular antique piece is upholstered as you dismantle it; take notes, and above all, save everything from the job until you're finished. Not only will this help in rebuilding, but you may be able to use some of the materials again, especially the padding.

Types of upholstered chair bottoms

Upholstered chair bottoms come in many construction modes, ranging from the barely padded variety to elaborate coiled spring arrangements. Common padding consists of upholstery fabric that's stretched over padding, such as horse hair or Excelsior, which is then placed over webbing or wood. Less common in antique chairs are coiled springs. Coils sit on webbing, are tied together, and are covered with padding, such as upholstering cotton, muslin and the fabric itself.

Of course, this is the way old chairs are supposed to be upholstered. Is this the condition in which your particular chair was acquired? If it's like some that I have seen, probably not. Typically, I've seen platform rockers with carpeting nailed where the upholstered seat should be, and wood panels have replaced webbing which rotted and was removed a long time ago. Often there is no seat at all!

Preliminary steps

Carefully remove the old upholstery; if you are going to redo an entire set of chairs, you may want to leave several of the chairs in various stages of seat dismantling to help you get them back together again. Making sketches on how corners are tacked in place may also be helpful. Saving old material makes it available for a pattern later and helps you order the right amount of material.

Make all chair repairs (Chapter 5) after removing upholstery, including removal of old webbing, if any. If you plan to strip and refinish the piece, you should do so before upholstering.

A repair task that may escape your attention is a problem with many old upholstered chairs. They have been reupholstered so many times that there is barely enough wood to get a new tack in; such tack holes, combined with dry wood and possibly termites, make it impossible to work on some antique chair frames. In these instances, you can either fill the old tack holes with the ends of round wooden toothpicks, after first removing *all* of the tacks, or you can make a new chair frame or portion thereof. To fill the holes, dip the end of a round toothpick into glue, push it into the larger holes first, and then break it off, flush with the lip of the hole. Allow the glue to dry before proceeding.

Adding new wood to defective frames, or even making a new frame, makes a lot of sense. Since this component doesn't generally show, the faithfulness-to-the-original issue cannot be raised, and you've got a structurally sound chair on which the new fabric will hang securely.

TOOLS. Correct tools consist of a tack hammer, webbing stretcher, tack puller, hot glue gun, stapler and a small crowbar. Tack hammers are indispensable: The hammer is curved to get at the concealed areas, is lightweight and less tiring to use, and the magnetized end picks up tacks and starts them. The webbing stretcher is a wooden, T-shaped tool, 8 in. (20 cm) long, with teeth at one end and padding at the other. You can really pull webbing across the opening with it, put the necessary pressure on it, and hold it while starting to tack the webbing in place.

The hot glue gun is useful for fastening upholstery in places where you can't get a tack hammer, and for fastening gimp. Staples have replaced tacks, especially

Professional upholstering tools and materials, left to right: webbing, webbing tool, tack puller, tacks and a magnetized tack hammer.

where super holding is not needed. Small crowbars are useful where heavily tacked webbing and upholstery can't be budged in any other manner.

MATERIALS. Starting from the bottom, you must have webbing; nearly all webbing needs to be replaced. It is a belt-shaped material that's 3½ in. (8.7 cm) wide, woven with jute. It is meant to be tough, since it supports either the coil springs or the padding. Ordinary burlap (hessian) covers the webbing if there are no springs, and it covers the springs if they are present.

String is tied to the springs both to hold them to the chair-seat rails and to each other. Padding in many antique chairs is typically horse hair or Excelsior. If it has not been ruined by moisture or by abuse and does not smell, plan to use it again. Cotton padding has been used and, of course, the modern padding is foam rubber. Place muslin over the padding, and put upholstery fabric over the muslin. If webbing is used, cambric goes under the chair bottom.

Have large quantities of tacks on hand. Buy them by their numbers: for webbing number 12 or 14, for fabric number 6 and for muslin number 4. Staples can also be used for the fabric and the muslin, and gimp can be fastened with a hot glue gun, but you can also buy gimp nails.

Upholstery fabric comes in all qualities, called grades. Grade D is the best, Grade A the cheapest. It will help to learn the grades and shop around a little; be sure to buy enough to finish your job.

Techniques

One technique to master is how to hold upholstery tacks in your mouth and how to remove them for tacking in place. Put a handful in your mouth. To dispense one at a time, turn the tack with your tongue so the head faces out. Let your tack hammer pull it out between your front teeth.

The steps in reupholstering are:

1. Tack webbing in place.

2. Cover webbing with burlap if there are no springs.

3. Replace springs and tie them.

4. Cover springs with burlap.

5. Put padding in place and tack.

6. Cover padding with muslin.

7. Install upholstery fabric.

8. Cover underside with cambric.

- *Step One.* Tack webbing to the underside of the seat rail, using number 12 or 14 tacks, if springs are present; otherwise, secure tacks to the top of the seat frame. Keep the webbing in a roll and use the same number of pieces in approximately the same location as before, unless the previous job was poorly done. Start tacking at one side of the frame, letting the webbing extend a few inches beyond the fastening line. Place your webbing stretcher in the free end next to you and pull it across the opening. Hold that end in place and put three tacks in it, fastening it to the frame. Cut the piece of webbing several inches beyond the fastening line.

Remove the tension on the webbing stretcher, and start with the next piece. Repeat this for every piece that runs from one side of the frame to the other. Tack the front-to-back strips into place, using the same motions. This time, however, weave over and under all the side-to-side webbing strips. Go back, double over the extended webbing ends, and put three more tacks through each end into the frame or rail.

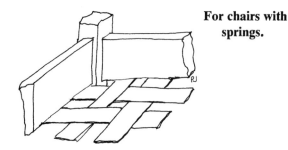

For chairs with springs.

One: Tack webbing in place.

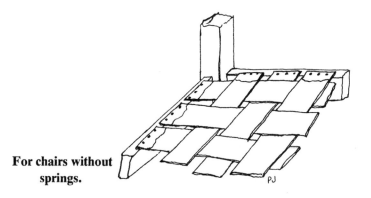

For chairs without springs.

● *Step Two.* If no springs are to be used, cover the webbing with a piece of burlap (hessian) that's been cut 1 in. (2.5 cm) over size. Double over the burlap edges, and tack or staple the piece to cover all the webbing. What you're doing is providing a seat for the padding.

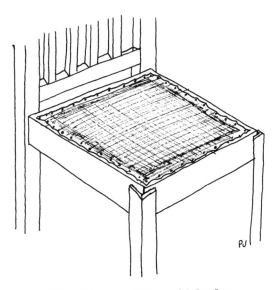

Two: Cover webbing with burlap.

● *Step Three.* Note any broken or missing springs before you start to tie them. Springs should sit on webbing intersections exactly as before, assuming it was a good job. Fasten them to these intersections with heavy needle and thread; three or four stitches, equally spaced on the spring bottom, should do it.

Springs should then be tied, using a square knot so as to provide a level surface and to keep springs in as upright a position as possible. Using a heavy cord, tack one end of the cord to the top of the back chair-seat rail, then to the top of the first spring in the back row, and across that spring (tying it again on the front side of that spring). Now tie the cord, keeping it in one piece, to the next spring, across it, tying it again, then to the third and so on to the front chair rail where it is again tacked. Take all front-to-back rows and tie them the same way. Finally, tie all side-to-side rows. When tying, exert minimal pressure on the springs.

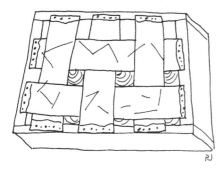

Three: Replace strings and tie them.

Tying detail.

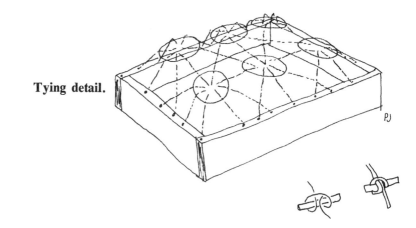

• *Step Four*. The springs are now to be covered with burlap. Stretch burlap tightly over the springs and staple it in place on the top of the side rails, right over the cord tyings.

• *Step Five*. Lay the padding over the springs, taking care to keep it spread evenly. Padding that goes on over webbing should also be smooth, especially cotton padding, which has a tendency to look lumpy. Foam padding should be shaped at its edges to retain the natural line of the chair's seat. A very sharp butcher knife will do a nice job of trimming foam-rubber blocks.

• *Step Six*. Covering the padding with muslin is not entirely necessary, in my opinion, but some experts recommend it. Pull the muslin snugly over the padding. A problem area is the edge where the slightest lump really shows. Pull, tuck and smooth it until you get a nice firm, smooth edge.

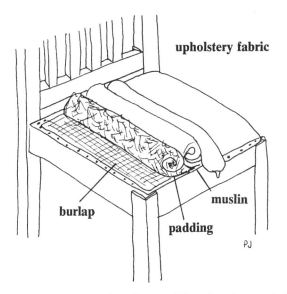

upholstery fabric

burlap

muslin

padding

PJ

Four: Cover springs with burlap. Five: Put padding in place and tack. Six: Cover padding with muslin. Seven: Install upholstery fabric.

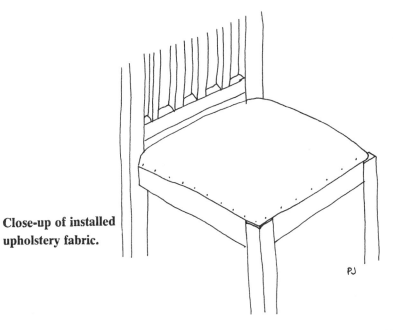

Close-up of installed
upholstery fabric.

PJ

• *Step Seven*. While all the previous steps are important, this is the one that shows. If previous reupholstering looks professional to you and you've not substantially changed the seat configuration, make your cuts, using the old fabric piece as a pattern, but be sure to allow yourself a little extra material so you can properly handle the job and make any adjustments that are necessary.

I fasten the front edge first, then pull everything to the rear and fasten that side, leaving a little working room at the corners. First one side is tacked or stapled, and a few tugs and pulls to the other side and it, too, is stapled in place. Watch not only for lumps, but for twisting and uneven patterns, and then start the corners.

Corners are always difficult for me. I generally use the technique of the previous upholsterer. For example, I ask myself whether the front, rather than the side, should be tucked first and where and how it was tacked. Often I have to try several approaches before one looks right.

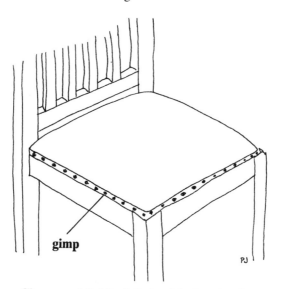

Close-up of finished chair with gimp in place.

• *Step Eight*. A complete job usually entails covering the underside of the chair seat with cambric. Cut a piece a little larger than needed, fold under the cut edges to prevent unravelling, and staple into place. Trim and apply gimp. Some antique chairs call for the use of gimp to hide the upholstery tacks that fasten the fabric. Gimp can be purchased in different colors by the yard. You can either nail it in place with gimp nails, or use the hot glue gun; I prefer the latter because there are already too many nails in antiques.

6 *Furniture Care and Touch-Up*

Museums carefully control the temperature and humidity of rooms which contain antiques, keep sunlight from shining on them, and try to keep the public from touching valuable antique pieces. The average antique owner, however, is often confused by the sometimes conflicting methods for furniture care given by experts in newspapers and magazine columns and antique dealers. The purpose of this chapter is to remove some of this confusion, tell you what the enemies of furniture care are, and assist you in patching surface defects.

Care Objectives

The care objectives of antique furniture collection are preserve (wood furniture can last a long time if it has been properly preserved), protect (from injury and abuse), and prevent. Much can be done in terms of prevention, since we can certainly anticipate some of the destruction that stalks our rooms. Chairs take quite a beating, especially those that are dragged under us over carpeting. Good chair glides fastened to the ends of chair legs go a long way in preventing their weakening. Trying to eliminate dust and sand, moving antiques away from direct sunlight, and installing humidifiers and dehumidifiers all assist in prevention.

The Enemies of Furniture

Environmental factors that can damage antiques and household furniture are dust, moisture, temperature, humidity, dryness, sunlight and atmospheric pollution. Poor housekeeping, plants, pets and careless use of antiques can also cause considerable damage.

Dust

Upon close examination, you will note that there are several kinds of dust. In the country, it is the dust of the fields, roads, plains and the mountains; most of it is loose topsoil. I call it "clean dust" because it's devoid of petrochemicals. There *is* grit in it, however. People living near the sea are subject to sea dust, the mixture of salt crystals and moist sand carried by wind and fog. Sea dust infiltrates even closed bookcases and can ruin books. In the city, dust is less the result of loose soil, and more the combination of that, plus steel-mill flue dust, soot and exhaust from cars and trucks. Add that to the petrochemicals of industry and refineries and you have a greasy, gritty dust.

Ordinary dust is destructive because the sharp edges of dust particles cut into and scratch fine furniture surfaces. Air conditioning and electrostatic dust collectors can cut down on the amount of dust in your home. Where sandstorms are frequent, keep doors and windows tightly shut, vacuum and dust often, and, if possible, install air conditioning and good humidification. Where sea dust is a problem, everything should be kept washed, dry and free from sea dust.

Moisture

Anyone living on or near a large body of water must contend with excessive moisture under normal living conditions. Stored objects really get the rough treatment: Mildew, termites and dry rot are the extremes. Ordinary dampness, however, can cause wood to warp, veneer to lift, inlays to loosen, drawers to swell and stick, and everything to smell damp and mouldy. Condensation is a further problem where moisture is great. Water vapor in the air collects on cool surfaces.

To combat dampness, install air conditioning, if possible, since moisture is taken out of the air, or use a dehumidifier if your area is already cool. If you have a crawl space under your house with no cellar floor on it, you can prevent some ground moisture from rising into your living quarters by laying heavy plastic drop cloths on the earth floor.

If there is a grey or white fuzzy mould on your furniture, it is mildew. Move any mildewed items into the air and sunshine, wash and then dry them. To prevent a reoccurrence, provide light and air, and dehumidification, if possible. If a storage area is the vicinity in which this fungus got started, provide air circulation and light. Otherwise, don't use the area.

If your antique piece has a damp smell, give it a very good washing, sunlight and air. If you note a damp smell when you are starting to strip the piece, use chemical stripper inside the piece as well as outside. To keep the piece from smelling, put a bar of pleasant-smelling soap in it, as you would in the drawers of a chest.

Termites and other insects

If you see termites—ants with white wings—flying about your place or crawling on your floor, call an exterminator, since termites can be very destructive and can cause considerable damage to wood furniture.

Moths will eat your upholstery, but mothproofing will protect your upholstery. Frequently rotate all upholstered pieces and vacuum them once a month.

Dryness

Dry heat is destructive because it can cause furniture to crack, split or buckle. It can also make veneer lift and small marquetry inlays to fall out.

If any of these problems are present in your antiques, your rooms probably need moisture. Such humidity can be readily provided by the use of humidifiers. If veneer is noticeably lifting, the antique piece may need to be resealed. To achieve this, you will probably have to strip the old finish and refinish the surface, as outlined in earlier chapters.

Sunlight

While sunlight is good for dampness and will help destroy and prevent mildew, too much of it can fade and dry furniture. Never place a fine antique piece where it can be baked by sunlight, since it doesn't take long for sunlight to bleach wood; the extreme heat dries out the natural oils in wood. Rather, place the piece where filtered sunlight can enhance its beauty.

Rotate furniture, especially if you own matching pairs. Dining tables should be turned occasionally to maintain even color; leaves should be taken out of storage and exposed; drop leaves should be raised occasionally; and folding table leaves should be opened periodically.

Atmospheric pollution

This form of pollution is almost impossible to control. Even country dwellers are now subjected to it, we are told, because pollution drifts in huge clouds over many miles from its source. Keeping windows and doors closed can help.

It is well known that façades of important, ancient buildings and temples in Athens and in Rome are being destroyed by the atmospheric pollution of cars and factories. Use air conditioners and electrostatic dust collectors, and clean regularly.

Pets

If you have lovely antiques and a cat that's primarily indoors, you might consider having the cat declawed to prevent furniture damage; most dogs can be trained not to chew on furniture.

Housekeeping

Proper housekeeping can eliminate potential damage to antiques, such as rings and stains.

Plants

Polyurethane finish on furniture can resist many types of damage that can result from the poor care of plants: leaks, dents, scratches, rings and lifting veneer (which has the potential to cause splits and warping). For though the pot may not leak, water that drips from leaves after watering will spot furniture.

If you must put a plant on an antique piece, place it in a guaranteed waterproof container and set it on a protective pad. When watering, either take the plant to the kitchen counter or be prepared to wipe up spilled water.

Perching on furniture

Exterior damage to the arms of wooden furniture pieces and interior damage to upholstered ones can result when people perch on furniture.

Furniture Care

Antique furniture care entails the same techniques as the care of all fine furniture, except that it may need more of it. The older the piece, the more fragile it is likely to be; some chairs should not be sat in at all.

Look at the feet of your chests and tables to see if they once had casters. If they did, try to pick up a set that matches the period of the piece. Both metal and wooden casters were used in the eighteenth and early nineteenth century, and the ceramic caster appeared with Victoriana. Wooden and metal casters reappeared in the twentieth century. Original casters can still be found in flea markets, and reproductions are available in specialty hardware and craft supply houses.

A common abuse of chests of drawers, buffets and sideboards is overloading drawers; once the runners or the drawer sides are worn or broken, expedient repair is necessary. Use desk pads on antique desk-writing surfaces and leather-topped tables, put coasters under drinking glasses, especially when it's humid, and cover ceramic pot bottoms with felt.

Dusting

Dust with one of the special dust cloths that both collect and settle dust, instead of most dust cloths, which merely push dust from one side of the surface to another. Vacuum cleaner dusters are also handy.

In general, avoid the spray products designed to aid dusting since you may be putting a foreign substance into the wood surface. Laying something on it might then do more to hold the dust than remove it.

Washing

Wood should be washed once in awhile; it is the best way to remove sea dust and is helpful where dryness is a problem. While sunlight and air will counteract mildew, washing must start the rehabilitation process.

When washing, use oil soap. To use it properly, make a small pail of soap solution by dissolving some of the soft soap in warm water. Fill a pail of warm water for rinsing and get three clean cloths: one for soap, one for rinse and one for drying. Wring out the cloth and cover the entire surface of the piece. Rinse immediately with a rinse rag that's been wrung out, and wipe the furniture surface dry so that it doesn't stay wet very long. For stubborn dirt, wipe the surface with grade 0000 steel wool that's been dipped in the soap solution. This process not only cleans, but it also gives your antique furniture a protective oil coating. Pieces cleaned in this way acquire a lovely patina and feel good to the touch.

Protective coatings

Oils and waxes are sticky and serve to hold dirt and dust; waxes tend to build up, particularly in areas of the piece not subject to regular use or cleaning. This buildup can discolor and mask the natural beauty of the wood grain. Furniture cream, I believe, provides sufficient protection to the well-finished antique and is washed off in the next washing; I therefore suggest that you wash your wood furniture twice a year and apply furniture cream after each washing.

The Art of Furniture Touch-Up

Before we turn to tools, materials and techniques used in the touch-up process, perhaps we should consider the old saying about leaving well enough alone. If you seriously question whether or not touching up (or "patching" as we often call it) will really improve the looks of your antique piece, perhaps you should leave it alone. Ideally, patching should be relatively invisible: The color and the light reflection of the patch should be identical with the furniture surface. Antiques, after all, are expected to have a few "care marks" as mute testimony to their long lives.

Touch-up and filling

Defects you can correct are scratches, dents, gouges, water marks and rings, white stains, candle wax, cigarette burns and blushing. Readily available materials are interior paint, stain, toothpaste, wax sticks, crayons, pecan nuts, and putty.

Deep gouges and nail holes can be corrected by filling them in with wax sticks, crayons or putty. Wax sticks come in a variety of shades and can be purchased at your local hardware dealer's, making for easy matching and availability. While they are easy to use, the material can be rubbed out of a filling because of its relative softness. Even more accessible, but less satisfactory, is the common crayon.

For deep holes, such as those made by a nail, use colored putty. However, putty's softness restricts its use only to very small-diameter holes. With these materials it is unnecessary to use common uncolored wood filler, because it does not take stain-coloring well.

Professional patching

The techniques and materials the furniture-store touch-up person carries are a little different. For touch-up, they have over 50 different colored powders which can be mixed with solvents to provide the exact color match. The powders can also be mixed for an infinite variety of colors. Their solvents come in at least three forms, one of which will dry in two minutes.

For filling, I use lacquer sticks—hard sticks of solid lacquer, available in a variety of shades. To apply the lacquer-stick fill, I use a burn-in knife heated in an electric knife heater. This melts the lacquer material so it can be put in the gouge or hole.

The skill of the professional lies in choosing the right color match, applying the patch correctly, and in sealing and finishing the patch so its light reflection is the same as the remainder of the surface. I will detail some of these techniques and materials as we explore common defects, presenting you with alternative approaches in patching.

MISSED SPOTS. In the refinishing process there were undoubtedly spots you missed or places where the stain didn't get properly absorbed, namely corners, deep carvings, incised designs, paint that's in nail holes, and gouges. You may have even missed staining in a wide-open place, such as the edge of a desktop. Take care of such missed spots after the sealing step.

The materials available to you are paint, stain and hardware-shop-variety touch-up. Buy touch-up paint that closely matches the sealed color of your antique piece and brush it in the light area, the corner that still has some paint pigment in it, or the rosette that is off-color. Sealer on surrounding surfaces allows you to easily wipe off excess touch-up without smearing it. Let it dry before brushing on the finish coat.

If the spot you missed should have been stained, try staining it with the original material. If that isn't properly absorbed by the wood, it's possible that either the sealer or the old finish is repelling it. Try sanding the spot while the stain is still wet. If that fails, wipe on a little stripper with a piece of steel wool and wipe clean with mineral spirits on a cloth; try staining the area again.

The best cover-up is touch-up powder mixed in a solvent. This material must be purchased in professionals' sets or kits and may cost more than you wish to spend. It does, however, cover sealers and poorly stripped spots.

SCRATCHES. Scratches are similar to missed spots except that they are more narrow and deep. You can use paint, stain, store touch-up and professional touch-up to correct scratches. Here, though, greater skill is called for, particularly if the scratch is prominent, as in the center of a Chippendale table. In such a place, not only must the color be an exact match, but the material cannot have a built-up look, and the light reflection of the patch must match that of surrounding surfaces.

First try rubbing the meat of half a pecan or a walnut into the scratch. For darker surfaces, try rubbing in a mixture of one teaspoon of instant coffee to two teaspoons water, and rub with the grain. If the piece with the problem is one that you recently refinished, try putting a little of the stain you used into the scratch, let it sit ten minutes, and gently wipe. If the piece has a "natural" finish, put some of the finish material you used into the scratch, let it set long enough to be absorbed, then wipe off the excess.

Professional restorers also have a product called scratch remover. When rubbed on a surface (which is first cleaned of old wax and polish), it does wonders in covering scratches.

GOUGES. Deeper scratches become gouges. To deal with a gouge, you have the choice of sanding, filling or touching them up. In general, avoid sanding out a gouge since sanding not only lightens adjacent wood, but it also causes the surface to become dished around that defect. If the gouge is really deep, it should be filled as if it were a hole. In just about all places on an antique piece, the wax stick is a good filler. The exception is the top, especially a desktop.

Since a gouge is generally an irregular shape, it is best to heat a knife on an alcohol burner and melt in a wax stick. Melting assures perfect packing of the depression. You can also put the material in cold by breaking off a bit and pushing it in the gouge with a screwdriver. For small, narrow gouges, you can rub the wax stick over the mark and fill it with shavings from the stick. Wipe off excess "wax" by rubbing the area with a rough cloth.

If the gouge is shallow, you may want to leave it, but remove any discoloration (they are typically very dark) and the attendant high visibility by touching up. Here a light color may well be called for to compensate for the almost black appearance of many gouges.

Finally, you may want to try the shellac stick, also known as the lacquer stick. You will need the most common colors, two burn-in knives and an electric knife heater or alcohol burner.

Lacquer is being applied onto a hot knife.

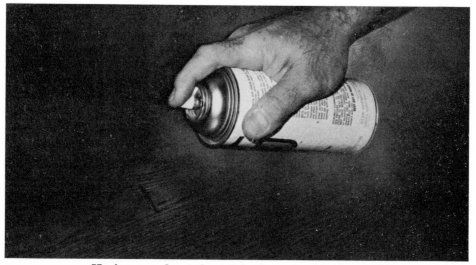

Having completed the patch, the author then seals it.

After heating the knives, pick up a little lacquer on one point of the knife and place it a little ahead of the gouge and pull it in with the knife, overfilling the damaged area. To smooth the convex fill, put some patch lubricant over the patch and adjacent surface. Take the other knife from the heater, putting your present one in to warm up again, and stroke the damaged area with enough pressure to fill it level. This move will also eliminate any air pockets and pick up excess lacquer. Wipe the area quickly with a rag, and clean off your knife, too.

As the patch is glossier in appearance than the wood around it, it is recommended that you patch before the finish coat. That coat, usually a satin finish, will cover the lacquer patch and give it the same light reflection as the rest of the surface. If, however, you are patching an already finished antique, you will have to spray the spot with a special finish protector. After that dries, spray on the proper sheen lacquer, a satin or a gloss.

DENTS. If a dent is too deep, it will have to be filled in the same manner as a gouge. Minor dents, however, can be steamed out, a process that works with soft woods. This process should be done before refinishing has started, but after the old finish has been stripped. Sealed wood cannot absorb the moisture that the steaming process uses to raise the wood grain.

To remove dents, place a wet rag over the defect and then a hot clothes iron, pressing hard at first to put steam into the wood. Let your iron, turned to low, sit on the rag from a few minutes to a few hours, checking progress periodically. If steaming doesn't work, you can always fill the dent if you think that will improve the situation, or leave it be and consider it a beauty mark.

WATER MARKS AND RINGS. It would appear that there are many cures and home remedies for water marks and rings. They range from rubbing paste wax on grade 0000 steel wool, working with the wood grain, to applying a few drops of lubricating or salad oil on the blemish and on a rottenstone, working with the grain of the wood. In any event, white rings are easy to remove.

The method that has worked for me is to rub the affected area carefully with a mixture of baking soda and toothpaste on a damp cloth. Rub with the grain and into a strong light, so that you can check your progress periodically, and then wash the area with oil soap. If the ring is still there, repeat the process. Dry the area and apply a furniture cream.

Water that has penetrated the old finish of an antique and has entered the wood surface will create a black ring. Stripping the old finish and sanding either the entire surface or sanding or bleaching just the rings may correct this defect in the wood. To bleach, brush a solution of oxalic acid crystals mixed according to directions in warm water, on the problem area. Another alternative, especially good for very small or partial black rings, is to touch up the defect after the sealing step in refinishing.

It is possible to sand out black rings, but sand only the ring. Sanding adjacent surfaces will lighten them, and you will then have to sand the entire surface to achieve tonal evenness. Sanding a circle necessitates sanding cross grain. Even though I have repeatedly said to sand *with* the grain, here I take exception to the rule. Avoid using too coarse a sandpaper when sanding cross grain. Frankly, I have had more success sanding out black rings than bleaching them. Perhaps you will, too, but since bleaching is easier, try that first.

CANDLE WAX. Often the end of a perfect evening is candle wax on your best antique. Allow it to harden overnight, or if you are in a rush, put an ice cube on the spill to firm it up. Use your fingers to remove as much wax as possible, then scrape gently with a dull knife or plastic cooking utensil. Follow that with a brisk rub of the area with furniture cream.

CIGARETTE BURNS. The trouble with cigarette burns is that they not only change the color of the wood, but they soften and dent the area as well. Sanding is of no avail because the dark color often goes pretty deep, and the softened wood is easy to remove. Soon you have a deep dish from your sanding efforts, and the wood is still black.

Short of redoing the whole surface, the best solution to the cigarette burn is to touch it up. Scratch out the really soft, ashlike damage with a sharp knife point; if you don't do that now, the damaged wood will probably crumble out later. If a really deep gouge has resulted, treat it as discussed previously; otherwise, a touch-up similar to that for a scratch should be employed. Keep in mind that you are trying to color-correct a deep, black mark; therefore, your touch-up color should be quite light. Daub in some sealer and finish material when the touch-up dries.

BLUSHING. Blushing is caused by moisture that has entered the finish, generally via condensation. The result is a sort of white haze. Before stripping a piece, try to remove the haze with super fine steel wood that's been dipped in linseed oil, and work it into the grain, rubbing back and forth with the grain. If this removes the blushing, wash off the oil and steel wool fuzz, and let the piece dry. Then, depending on the condition of the finish, you will want to either seal and finish the affected surface, or just put some furniture cream on it. By utilizing this process, you have just saved yourself a stripping job.

Serious hazing may not be removed in this manner, however. In that unfortunate event, I'm afraid that you will have to strip the piece, or at least the affected surface.

7   *How Antique Furniture Was Made*

Before you dive into your project, it will be helpful to have some knowledge of furniture woods, of furniture finishes and construction. Actually, information on antique furniture construction is quite scanty, and many of us in the trade have had to learn through experience. Nevertheless, over the years, experience and research have taught me much. What follows is a brief but handy collection of all the necessary basic information.

Common Woods Used in Antiques

Knowing wood species and their characteristics is important not only for refinishing and repairing antiques but also for dating them. For example, if you knew the approximate dates for the age of mahogany or oak, you'd be able to assign your particular furniture piece a "loose" (but probably fairly accurate) place in history.

Early American cabinetmakers are said to have used about 25 different woods, two-thirds of which were "hard" and the remainder "soft." About ten species, such as amboyna, applewood, holly and pear, were rare and used in rather limited amounts. The more commonly used varieties were ash, basswood, birch, butternut, cherry (black), chestnut, hickory, mahogany, maple, oak, pine, rosewood, whitewood (poplar) and walnut.

The Victorian period is often considered the era of black walnut and rosewood. While walnut and rosewood were certainly popular for fine-furniture manufacture, altogether 12 different woods were consistently in use, including butternut, ash, maple, oak, pine, mahogany and cherry.

The Victorian period was followed by what some refer to as the Golden Oak period and what I prefer to think of as Late Victorian. You would think this period concentrated on red and white oak exclusively. Actually it didn't. Much ash found its way into Golden Oak, adding to the confusion of dealers and collectors today.

Dovetailing with Golden Oak, Art Nouveau was a period high in style but short in duration. Walnut and rosewood were the main furniture construction materials, although the period's curvilinear designs demanded the increasing appearance of metals.

Oak was the sole material of Mission furniture, which followed, and is often added to the name Mission, becoming Mission Oak.

Art Deco furniture continued the use of metal introduced by Art Nouveau. The metals, however, were polished chrome and brass (in contrast to the former satin finishes), and they advanced from being mere decoration to being the sole construction material for some pieces. Bleached, blond, painted and natural veneers replaced the solid materials which had dominated the scene for over a century. Some rather exotic materials also were introduced, such as lemonwood, boxwood, vermilion (Indian padauk) and Burmese amboyna.

The William and Mary revival (as I call it), or Depression furniture of the Twenties and early Thirties, concentrated on walnut, although oak, poplar and basswood continued to be in use. (The latter two were stained walnut to imitate the more expensive wood.) And the interest in Early American that developed in the Thirties once again placed great interest on maple.

Today, furniture makes use of most of the veneers of known woods. Solid pieces are still made of pine, maple and oak. Veneers, depending on the grade of furniture, are rare or plentiful, expensive and cheap. They're glued to a core of cheap oak, maple, birch in the case of better furniture, and particle board and furniture plywood in the case of cheaper grades.

Wood Characteristics

Each kind of wood has a set of characteristics that distinguishes it from another species. Usually, each species differs considerably, but at times several can be confusingly similar, and the ways in which furniture manufacturers use them further complicate identification.

For example, I recently restored an early twentieth-century highboy chest which was very cleverly made of ash and oak. Small elements needing a material for strength were made of oak, whereas the large expanses were made of the cheaper, yet decorative, ash. Careful examination is necessary to notice the subtle differences.

ASH. Ash has a grain, texture and finished color of light brown with yellowish veins similar to that of oak. Ash differs in having unpronounced pores, a medium (rather than hard) density and always has an irregular or wavy grain. In the mid-seventeenth century, it was used for turned, Windsor and country chairs. Due to its desirable smell, ash was fitted to the interiors of drawers and wardrobes.

In the late Victorian period, ash returned as the principal wood for bedroom suites. Today, its natural light-cream color often is identified as Golden Oak by unknowing antiques dealers and unsuspecting buyers.

The restored Mission Oak staircase ballusters and newel posts have been restored, along with a Mission Oak hall tree (c. 1910) and serve as an elegant entry to a home.

BASSWOOD. This is a softwood that's light and straight-grained. It is chiefly used for interior sections such as drawer bottoms and backs, and the backboards of case pieces in both Colonial and Victorian times. In the eighteenth century, entire painted chests, highboys and desks were made of basswood by country cabinetmakers. Basswood acquires a brownish-yellow tone in the finished state.

BIRCH. Birch is a very heavy, very strong and hard (though softer than oak), close-grained wood, possessing an even, fine texture and a cream or light brown color that's tinged with red. Its grain pattern is typically plain, but often curly. Thus being very similar to maple, it is often mistaken for maple. Because it can be curly (and therefore decorative) and takes a high polish, birch was used for tabletops in Colonial times, as well as for skirts and drawer fronts of all-birch pieces.

In Victorian times birch was sometimes stained, with varying results, to resemble mahogany and walnut. More frequently it was polished unstained and used as a veneer on bedroom furniture. A popular material for cheap, mass-produced items, it found its way into plywood manufacture after 1890.

BUTTERNUT. Sometimes called "white walnut," but of a finer texture, butternut is a hard, close-grained, very light-brown wood, having a soft density. Although not widely used in Colonial times except for an occasional Queen Anne highboy, butternut was used by nineteenth-century cabinetmakers in the Midwest, until about 1865. These craftsmen made chests of drawers, tables, desks, cupboards and similar pieces with it.

CHERRY. Extensively used in both Colonial and Victorian America because of its beauty, this species is a medium-to-hard density wood with a reddish brown color when finished. Sometimes it's confused with mahogany because cherry can also be close-grained as well as curly, similar to the roey mahogany crotch grain. Interestingly, modern authorities give cherry a beauty rating of one, while mahogany gets only a two.

Beginning in the eighteenth century, Connecticut cabinetmakers used cherry for their butterfly tables. By about 1770 it was being substituted for mahogany in tables, chairs, chests, highboys and other furniture. During the Chippendale, Hepplewhite, Queen Anne, Sheraton and Empire periods, it was used extensively. Some Boston rocker arms are of cherrywood, and in the late Victorian era, some better grades of Eastlake furniture used cherry.

CHESTNUT. A medium-density wood, chestnut is somewhat similar to oak, being a warm, mellow, brownish yellow color when finished. It was mostly used for concealed structural elements of chests of drawers, beds and sofa frames during post-Colonial times. However, in Eastlake Victorian furniture, factories featured it on their popular-priced beds and bedroom suites.

Natural birch

WHITEWOOD. Also known as poplar, yellow poplar and the tulip tree, this type of wood is sometimes canary colored, with a slight greenish cast. Because it is a readily available softwood, and therefore cheap, it was used for backboards and structural pieces in Early America. Nonetheless, some Windsor chair seats, blanket chests, cupboards and dressers were made of whitewood until about 1770. Very rare are William and Mary highboys made of poplar.

Whitewood does not appear in Victoriana. However, it made its debut once again in the twentieth century in inexpensive cupboards, both painted and stained, and in other case goods well into the Twenties. It was also used in less expensive William and Mary revival pieces when it was stained to match and imitate walnut.

117

HICKORY. Hickory is a strong, heavy wood that was widely used in Early America for Windsor and Boston rocker spindles because of the tenacity of its fibre. Its color is white to cream with inconspicuous fine brown lines and tan heartwood. Although unpopular in Victorian times, today it is widely in use as a furniture veneer because of its hard density, availability, price and beauty.

MAHOGANY. Because of its strength, hardness, firm texture and roey grain, mahogany appeared early as the wood from which fine furniture was made. Mahogany varies from deep reddish brown to red with brown undertones. It dominated the furniture scene from 1750 to 1840, representing the Chippendale, Hepplewhite, Sheraton and Empire periods with fine examples. The crotch grain of the African mahogany tree was prized early on as a highly decorative veneer and continued to be used through the Empire period. As these trees sometimes grew to ten feet in diameter, Early American table leaves of mahogany are almost always in one piece.

Victorian furniture featured mahogany, most notably for chairs, bedposts, table-tops and legs, and veneers. San Domingan mahogany was hard and dark in color. Although Cuban mahogany also was dark, it tended to show more figure. Mahogany from Honduras was lighter, easier to work, and superior to West African mahogany, but similar in color and texture.

Much modern furniture utilizes mahogany veneers. The final color of mahogany depends upon the finishing it receives. Today, its natural color most often is a pale reddish brown.

MAPLE. Although maple is usually straight-grained, it can also be birdseye, curly, fiddleback, blistered, and even quilted. Characteristically heavy, hard, strong, close-grained, tough and stiff, it can be worked with ease and doesn't warp easily. Naturally whitish when finished, its color varies from a light, brownish yellow to a rich amber.

Straight-grained maple was used by American cabinetmakers from 1650; 50 years later, curly maple began to be used for decorative parts and entire pieces. Maple also was used as a substitute for satinwood.

Formerly, maple was scorned by antiques authorities because it was the cheap material (along with pine and walnut), and because nameless, rural cabinetmakers fashioned it into furniture destined for poorer homes. Today, these humble maple pieces, such as corner cupboards, cradles, four-poster beds and gate-legged tables have become very desirable and valuable.

As a veneer, maple was popular in early, factory-made pieces, chiefly chests of drawers, and as interior fittings of davenports to contrast with the darker woods of the exterior.

OAK. The natural color of oak ranges from light brown with a greyish tinge in the heartwood to shades of ochre in the sapwood. In most oak antique furniture, the color is a warm brown. Oak has a pronounced long ray and a pin-stripped figure in the rift cut. Plain slicing gives it a pattern of plain strips and leafy grain. Occasionally there are crotches with swirls and burls. Quarter-sawing of oak, principally a process of the mid-nineteenth century to the early twentieth, gave oak a tiger pattern, greatly enhancing its beauty.

Though hard and heavy, oak has had an uneven history. Seventeenth-century furniture, principally Puritan-style chests, court cupboards, chair spindles and trestle table bases, were made of oak until about 1720.

After that year oak became principally a structural material for 150 years. Its next big appearance was in the solid-oak Eastlake Victorian pieces, and in England oak was preferred in hall, dining and library furniture. There it was finished only by rubbing polish in it and keeping it polished.

From the Eastlake period, oak increased in popularity and became the principal material in Golden Oak and Mission Oak pieces. Today, oak, such as ranch oak, is in very common use.

WALNUT. The popularity of American walnut over the years is due to many factors, the most outstanding being that this one species produces a greater variety of figures than any other. Authorities rate its beauty as 1.

This species is very strong for its weight, exceptionally stable and easily worked. And, until modern times, it has been easily and cheaply available. As to color, it ranges from a light greyish-brown to a dark purplish brown; the red Virginia walnut in early Queen Anne and Chippendale highboys and the black walnut in high Victorian pieces are examples of color ranges.

The popularity of walnut waned as oak took over in the late Victorian period. It did not appear until briefly in the Art Nouveau movement, and then much later in the William and Mary revival style. Today walnut is a popular and expensive wood, found mostly as a veneer; the oiled walnut of the late Fifties and Sixties were popular examples of this wood's contemporary usage.

ROSEWOOD. Also known as purplewood, it is red-purplish in color when finished, and dark purple to ebony in nature. Rosewood is a very hard, firm, close-texture wood that stands up exceptionally well under all conditions. Its pattern is small-to-medium pores in wavy lines. It has apparently always been valuable, and its use was generally limited to veneer. It was first used as veneer for inlay panels, banding and other details on Hepplewhite mahogany pieces, and on Sheraton and Empire pieces.

In the first 25 years of the Victorian period, much of the elaborate furniture, well-illustrated in the Belter laminated pieces, was made of rosewood veneer. Some Art Nouveau pieces were made of solid rosewood and rosewood veneer. Today rosewood veneer is a material reserved for top-of-the line furniture.

Walnut

Brazilian rosewood

Cherry

African-striped mahogany

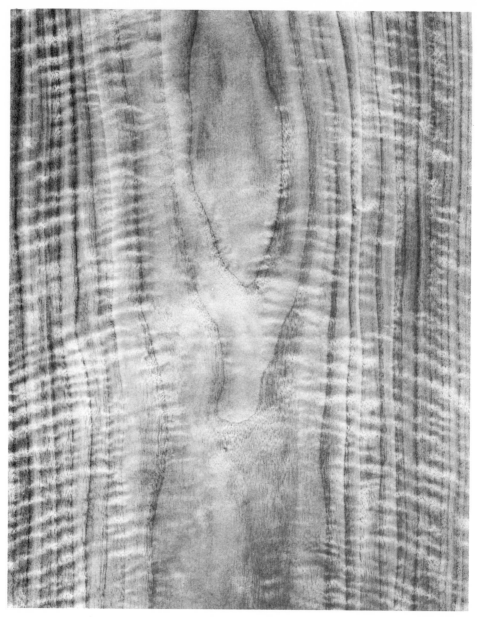

Black walnut

PINE. The first thing one should know about pine is that at least three species were used in the making of old furniture: Southern hard, white and Northern yellow. Today there is also Idaho white, Northern white, ponderosa sugar white, and Southern yellow in the United States and ocote in parts of Mexico and Central America and parana pine in South America. But to simplify matters, the most common pine in antiques is good old white pine.

Sometimes called "pumpkin pine," white pine is a straight-grained softwood available in wide knot-free boards. In Colonial and Early America, it was used for backboards, drawer sides, the backs and bottoms of case pieces, as well as for the tops of simple tables and four-poster bed headboards. Cupboards and other simple country pieces were made of white pine, as well as painted Pennsylvania Dutch furniture. Windsor and Boston rocker seats were made of pine, as were gilded mirror frames of the Chippendale period.

Pine also found extensive use as carcass wood and as core wood for veneer tables. Many mahogany veneer tables, for example, have white pine cores. Later, in Victorian times, vast quantities of cottage furniture were manufactured from pine.

Original Furniture Finishes

You may be fortunate enough to have an antique piece with its original finish still intact. What is more likely is that it has been refinished or covered over sometime during its long existence. It is helpful in restoring antiques to know what the probable finish was, since you will then understand how to remove it, if that becomes necessary, and what to replace it with. Awareness of old finishes can also help in dating antiques.

Common antique furniture finishes

Finishes commonly used by original manufacturers, cabinetmakers and re-finishers were shellac, stain (dyes and other coloring), lacquer, varnish, polyurethane and paint. Wax, various polishes and fuming were less commonly used.

You can tell whether or not a particular piece has been finished—or refinished over the original finish—with a visual inspection. Finish unevenness (runs and drippings) indicates the piece has been refinished. Look for this on the underedge of a table, the interior backs of cases or the underedge of chair stretchers. If the restoration job was a poor one, the finish probably is rough to the touch; if the surfaces are smooth, chances are that no new finish has been applied.

When chips, nicks or cracks appear to have been covered up, the piece has been refinished. Check carvings to see whether they are sharply delineated or rounded and dull, as if they had been sanded or scraped. Sharpness indicates no prior refinishing. Finally, if an Empire piece is painted but paint wasn't used as the finish for this style or period (which it wasn't), the piece has been refinished.

BARE WOOD. Some Early American country or primitive furniture made by local cabinetmakers often received no finish other than some beeswax or polish. But if you found such an early example, quite likely all of the old "nonfinish" would be worn off or covered up with paint or varnish.

SHELLAC. Up until the beginning of the Victorian era, nearly all clear finishes on furniture were shellac. But shellac is a very unsatisfactory finish because it absorbs moisture and darkens with age; it turns white when water is left on it. Because alcohol is the solvent of shellac, alcohol dissolves shellac. To test for the presence of shellac, put some denatured alcohol on a rag and wipe some hidden corner of the piece. If the finish dissolves, it's shellac.

STAINS. Generally, Early American furniture was sealed over raw wood for a clear finish, or it was painted. The sealer resulted in a darkened tone and richness of grain.

There was, though, some staining of wood. We are told that old English walnut was stained and that mahogany was often artificially reddened in the latter part of the Empire period. The sapwoods of walnut, rosewood and satinwood were often toned up for an even tonal appearance.

The practice of staining furniture increased in the nineteenth century. Most significant was the Victorian black walnut appearance achieved by treating the furniture with an acid wash before varnishing or shellacking. From about 1840 to 1870, some furniture designed chiefly for the parlour and the boudoir was finished with a fine black lacquer and then decorated. Such lacquered pieces were factory-made, finished with a dense black ground coat, and stencilled in gilt, combined with painted birds or flowers.

In the Golden Oak period, furniture was stained in the factory to achieve a lighter-than-natural oak color, and in the Mission Oak period that followed, wood that was not fumed (which was most of it) was stained to match the dark, almost Flemish black color of the fuming process.

In this late Victorian period, cheaper pieces made from poplar, pine and basswood were dyed or filled to imitate mahogany. This dye is impossible to remove in normal furniture stripping. So if you are attempting to refinish such a piece, about the best you can hope for is a return to mahogany.

A series of stains, both analine and oil, varnish stains and stains mixed with lacquer appeared in the twentieth century. Matching different wood varieties became a science; furniture was produced that combined many different woods—both solid pieces and veneers—that appeared to be from the same tree and log.

A refinishing note on stain: Once a piece of furniture has been stained, the *natural* color of the wood species has been changed—forever. You will never get it "natural."

PAINT. It was the custom at different times in the United States to paint the entire surface of various furniture pieces, especially chairs. Some pieces have been covered with many layers of paint. In preserving the original coat because of a possible finely painted design, great care must be taken in removing subsequent paint. Also, paint may cover a multitude of defects and a rather careless matching of wood species by the original cabinetmaker.

In buying a painted antique, it is best to try to scrape off some of the paint. If it is new, it will be soft and come off more easily; if it is old, it will be hard and come off like powder. Such a test may also reveal the kind of wood from which the piece was made.

While much Early American furniture was painted (black and red were most popular), practically the only painted pieces in the Victorian period were of the Cottage style. This style was a Victorian substyle, produced in huge volume from 1845 to 1890. Made of pine, painted furniture was distributed mostly through mail order. Because it resembled Early American styles, fakery resulted when enterprising individuals stripped off the original paint and the applied moulding, beat up the piece a little, stained it an antique brown, and sold it as Early American.

Practically any other Victorian piece that you run across that is painted does not have the original patina. Painted furniture has made brief appearances in more recent times, much of it being confined to kitchen cabinets, some bedroom suites and the Art Deco movement pieces (which often were painted bright colors). A classic example is a chair by Gerrit Rietveld, a sort of neo-plasticism design. The back vertical plane is red, and the intersecting horizontal planes represented by the arms, seat and stretchers are blue. The chair legs are black and the various component piece ends are yellow. Restoration of such a piece should follow the designer's original intent.

VARNISH. Historically, varnish is first mentioned in connection with French varnish developed by the four Martin brothers, in business in Paris from about 1725 to 1765. Paraphrased "Martin's Varnish," it is said to have had a fine lustre to it which compared well to Chinese and Japanese products, and was considered a lacquer product at that time.

Despite its early introduction, varnish was not used much until the Victorian period, and even then it was mostly used on hand-crafted pieces. Shellac, by now the so-called "tough" shellac, continued in use by furniture manufacturers until it was replaced by lacquer and polyurethane.

Perhaps the limited use of varnish was due to its slow-drying nature, which did not lend itself to the factory production of furniture of the time. It was, and is, far superior to shellac in that it resists everything. Since it cannot be dissolved (as shellac and lacquer can), it must be removed by a paint-and-varnish remover.

Though few original furniture pieces—both old and new—were finished in varnish, the collector is more than likely to run into one since most furniture restoration has entailed varnish. However, that is changing as more and more refinishing is being done with lacquer.

LACQUER. Lacquer was originally a kind of varnish made in China and Japan from the sap of the gum tree. Much lacquered work was imported by England starting about 1675, and the process called "Japanning" was adopted and employed in furniture production by English cabinetmakers until 1800. Little American-made furniture was finished in this manner, but undoubtedly many imports by the colonies included lacquered pieces.

Today all furniture is finished with lacquer, a trend which probably began at the beginning of the century in some shops. Lacquer dries almost the minute it hits the furniture surface, thus lending itself to the application of many coats and to a speeded-up production line. Its disadvantage is that it cracks when it dries, due to its brittle nature, and does not always resist alcohol.

To tell whether or not your furniture is finished with lacquer, place some lacquer thinner on a rag and wipe a scuffed or worn part of the furniture surface. If it's lacquer, it will dry in a few minutes, and the surface will appear smooth and glossy again.

WAX. Wax was used by some cabinetmakers on country pieces and on some oak pieces in Victorian England. It provides a seal from the elements and is probably preferable to shellac. Its disadvantage is that it wears and washes off surfaces and has to be replaced.

FUMING. Fuming is considered the authentic color of Mission Oak furniture, a sort of Flemish black to dark oak to English oak. Furniture was subjected to the fumes of ammonia derived from a solution listed as 880-ammonia. While it is possible to do the same thing, I understand that you can achieve the same color by brushing on a solution of 880-ammonia. I have matched Mission Oak color by mixing a dark stain and brushing it on.

MILK PAINT. Milk paint was made by reducing milk to the consistency of paint and mixing it with animal blood. A milk-painted piece is tough and wears well. The finish is almost impossible to remove, although I have succeeded in doing so with great difficulty.

To duplicate milk paint, mix powdered milk in water with a paint thickness and add tint for color.

Antique Furniture Construction

While all of the early construction decoration and detail was hand-carved, nearly all of the later antique ornamentation found in Victorian pieces was machine-generated. The same holds true for furniture building. Machine cutting was increasingly employed in the Victorian era until all furniture was made by machine. Let's consider a Frank Lloyd Wright chair, a Beidermeier chest of drawers, a round oak table and a Gothic Victorian wardrobe.

A close-up view of the author shows him in the process of restoring a chair from the Frank Lloyd Wright Studio. The chair has Mission-style spindles (i.e., spindles that are straight and square).

Chairs

The chair in the illustration is one of eight that Frank Lloyd Wright and his family used from about 1890 to 1909. The chair-back uprights are typically an extension of the rear legs, forming one element. The back uprights in this chair are held together by the top rail and a crossbar just above the seat rail, which also holds the back together. In this illustration the spindles are Mission style (straight and square) and connect the top rail and the crossbar. The other possible chair-back component is the splat which is wider and flatter than the spindle.

The front legs are connected by the front seat rail, which in turn is connected to the back by the two side seat rails. The stretchers, in this instance the H-shape, further support the legs. The leather-upholstered seat fits into the L-shaped seat rails and is held by two wood screws, front and back. Victorian finials crown the back uprights, illustrating the transitional nature from Victorian to Mission.

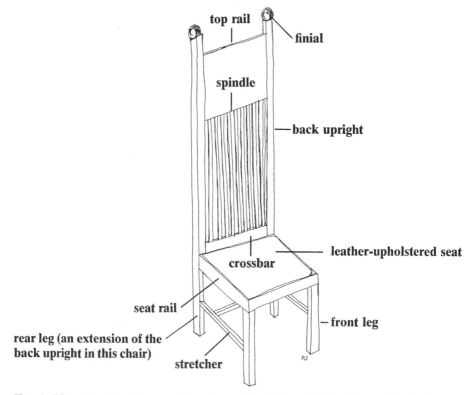

Frank Lloyd Wright family dining side chair (c. 1890), Frank Lloyd Wright Home and Studio, Oak Park, Illinois

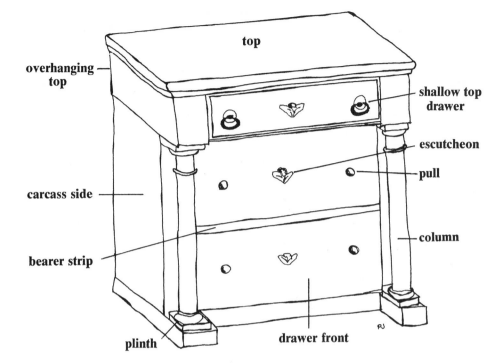

Biedermeier chest, German Empire period (c. 1840)

Chest of drawers

The major components of a chest are the top, carcass, backboard and drawers. The chest illustrated is a Beidermeier from the German Empire period (c. 1840). While it now has only a pine top, at one time there was probably a marble top. The carcass is of solid wood construction, covered with a ⅛-in. (3-mm)-thick pearwood veneer, as are the drawer fronts. The veneer covering the drawer fronts is of two matching pieces. Drawers are separated by bearer strips and are supported by runners on which the sides slide. The back is a soft wood, comprised of lap-joined vertical boards.

This chest, so typical of the Empire period, has an overhanging top and two front columns "supporting" it and resting on plinths. The top drawer is considered shallow. Drawer bottoms are bevelled by hand-planing, and the dovetails are hand-cut, narrow and few in number. They join the drawer sides to the fronts. Drawer keyholes are centered in escutcheons.

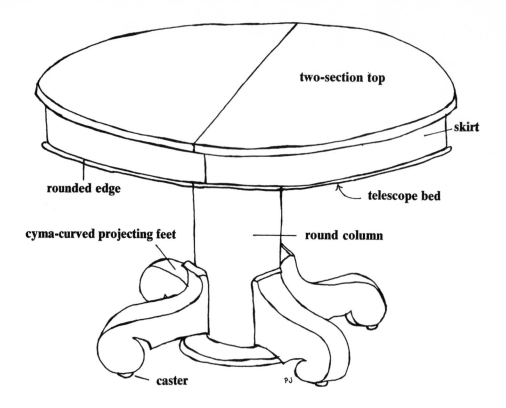

two-section top

skirt

rounded edge

telescope bed

cyma-curved projecting feet

round column

caster

PJ

Round Oak (pedestal extension) table

As most round dining tables were manufactured in the early Mission, Golden Oak and late Victorian periods, they were usually made of oak (the most popular material of those times), hence the term "round oak." While many such tables are of veneer construction, this particular one has a solid, quarter-sawed oak top, consisting of a number of boards glued together and held by dowels. The skirt and the edge moulding is also solid oak that has been shaped into a half circle.

This table is 54 in. (137 cm) in diameter and can hold only two leaves, since the round pedestal column does not split for the support needed for more leaves. The column is covered with oak veneer, but the cyma-curved projecting feet are solid oak. As with most extension tables, this one features a concealed telescopic bed for extension leaves. Other round oak tables come in widths of 36 in. (91 cm), 44 in. (112 cm) and 48 in. (122 cm). Pedestals on some models split and move with the table as it is extended.

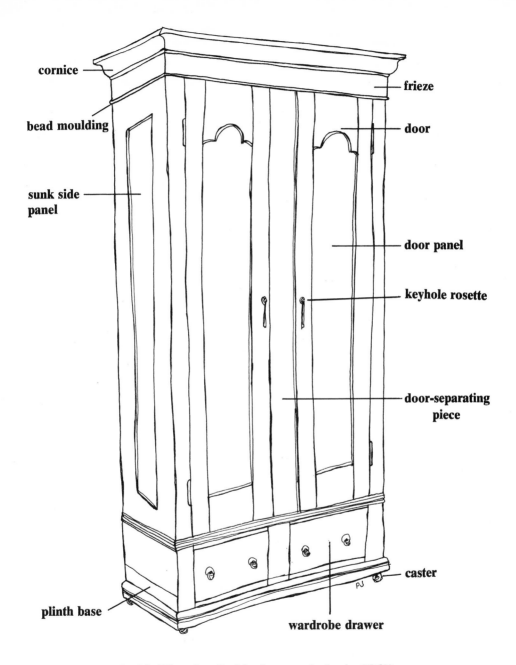

cornice

frieze

bead moulding

door

sunk side
panel

door panel

keyhole rosette

door-separating
piece

caster

plinth base

wardrobe drawer

Gothic Victorian double-door wardrobe (c. 1860)

Wardrobe

The wardrobe shown on page 131 is nearly identical to the one in the home that Abraham Lincoln's family occupied in Springfield, Illinois, just before he became president. It is a Gothic Victorian, identifiable by the arched door panels. Since built-in clothes closets were few and small at that time, the wardrobe was a necessary piece of furniture for clothes storing. Such wardrobes continued to be popular well into the 1880's.

The illustrated wardrobe is tall and made of solid walnut. It comes apart in seven pieces to facilitate moving: the top, two doors, vertical lapjointed backboard, two side pieces and the base. It features a bold convex/concave, overhanging bevelled cornice with square corners. Beneath this is a plain frieze about 6 in. (15 cm) high, defined top and bottom by a narrow band of bead moulding.

Both the doors and the sides have one-piece solid walnut sunken panels. Door hinges are the hang, pin-in-hole variety, making their removal easy. Keyholes are framed in walnut rosettes. There are two wardrobe drawers, nailed and not dovetailed, and the base in which they are located appears to rest on a plinth, but indeed does not. The large casters are made of cast-iron.

8   *What Antique Furniture Looks Like*

Knowledge of identifiable style characteristics of antiques and construction details will assist you in repairing and refinishing your antiques and collectibles, and enable you to make a wise purchase.

Early American Furniture

In Colonial and Early America, the furniture—or more accurately the cabinet-maker industry—operated a type of three-track system. On the first two tracks there was the nameless country craftsman making tables, chairs and other pieces for farm families and the less affluent, using local woods and employing local craftsmen. Such pieces have been divided by authorities into "country" and "primitive." "Country" pieces were the craftsman's interpretation of the fashionable English designs, which did, however, remain close to the pattern books then being published. "Primitive" furniture, in contrast, was much less pure, since it was a combination of various styles of that time—and previous styles—making the pieces very difficult to date.

On track three were the "high style" English designs: Queen Anne, Chippendale, Hepplewhite and Sheraton. These designs have been well documented, both as to their origin and date. High-style pieces were copied from pattern books by city cabinetmakers for their wealthy customers. A good well-known illustration of such a cabinetmaker is Duncan Phyfe, who copied such famous stylists as Thomas Chippendale and Thomas Sheraton of London.

We will first look at the recognized high styles and then turn to country and primitive pieces.

Styles before 1725

There were two basic antique furniture styles in Colonial America before 1725, the year the Queen Anne style was introduced. They are the Puritan style (also called "Stuart" and based on the English "Jacobean"), made from about 1600 to 1690, and William and Mary, made from 1690 to 1720. As our population was very small and the homes sparsely furnished, very few original pieces from this period have survived.

Puritan and Stuart furniture pieces were massive and heavy. Puritan was mostly wainscot; that is, it was constructed to fit into or against a wall, and is considered architectural in mass. Case pieces had no legs or feet. Made of oak combined with pine, the principal pieces are court and press cupboards, dower chests, wainscot and turned armchairs, slat-backed joined stools and trestle tables.

Stuart chests were made of six very wide boards, giving them the label "six-board chests." Another classic example of this style is the Carver and Brewster chair dichotomy. They are upright turned armchairs, having either rushed or splint seats. The only difference is that the Brewster has a double row of back spindles, and the Carver has a single row. They were not only very popular in their day, but were copied by the thousands in Victorian times.

William and Mary furniture designs took pieces away from the wainscotted wall, significantly lightened them, put legs on them and introduced walnut and maple woods. Furniture legs, either spiral or trumpet-turned, were 20 inches (51 cm) long. It has been said that a room decorated with William and Mary pieces looks like a forest of wooden legs. Feet were also important. Case pieces and others had bulbous or turnip-shaped feet. Teardrop pulls were introduced and some maple pieces were lacquered in the Chinese manner.

Newly introduced furniture pieces were highboys, lowboys, carved high-back chairs with caned back panels and seats, slant-top desks, and gate-leg, butterfly and tavern tables. The William and Mary era also brought in the first really comfortable chair, the upholstered easy chair.

Queen Anne (1720–1750)

Queen Anne is probably just as important as a "reproduction" style as it is an original. It has been very popular over the years, perhaps because of Queen Anne's distinctive cabriole legs and pad feet.

This design continued the trend towards lightness and away from architectural integration present in Puritan furniture. Walnut wood continued to be popular, although maple was used and cherry was first introduced. Quick identification of Queen Anne can be made by noting the carved scallop-shell motif carved on cabriole leg knees, the fan and sunburst carvings on small central drawers of highboys, and the H-hinge found on cabinet doors.

Construction consisted of distinctive cabriole legs, Dutch feet (a plain, slightly curved foot), a vased-shaped chair-back splat, and tall case pieces topped with urns or flame finials. All pieces are delicately proportioned. All chairs had a curved top rail, and the splat rests on the seat rail rather than a crossbar. The later the Queen Anne chair, the more likely that you'll find stretchers (a combination H configuration with a connecting piece between the back legs).

Queen Anne settee

Chippendale (1750-1785)

As in the Queen Anne style, Chippendale has been extensively reproduced since its introduction. It is a rococo extension of its predecessor which switched the wood emphasis from walnut to mahogany, though some walnut Chippendale was made. While the cabriole leg continued, the foot became a deeply carved claw and ball, and stretchers were omitted. One can see the beginnings of the Sheraton style here with the development of the fluted or reeded straight-square leg terminating in the square foot. Case goods now had a bowed front carcass and pilasters (half columns) appeared. Bail handles of brass became an important part of the decor.

Pieces introduced by Thomas Chippendale are chests-on-chests, tilt-top tables, kneehole writing tables, and block-front (kettle base) furniture. Still more comfort was provided by the large upholstered sofa he designed. Some of England's finest antique furniture, as well as furniture of the United States, comes from this period.

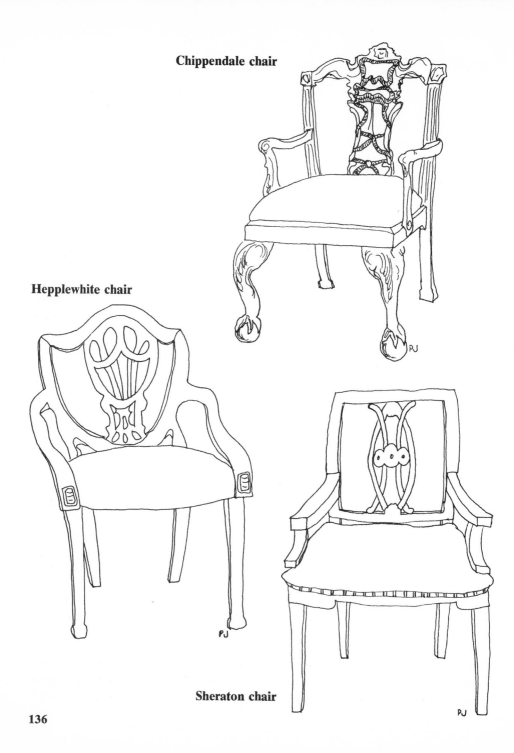

Chippendale chair

Hepplewhite chair

Sheraton chair

Hepplewhite (1785-1800)

The outstanding structural characteristics of this period are slender tapering legs, straight perpendicular lines, horizontal curves, and the colorful use of contrasting inlay and veneer. Feet were now French, a slightly outswept bracket foot always combined with a valenced skirt. The peak of delicacy was achieved with this style. From this point it is felt that furniture styles descended to the bulk and heaviness of the Early and High Victorian period.

Hepplewhite chairs are recognizable for their height, back configuration and legs. They are a standard 37 in. (94 cm) tall; backs are shaped as shields, ovals, hearts or wheels, and they don't touch the seat at all. Legs are delicately carved, straight and tapered; a complete departure from the heavier Chippendale and still heavier-appearing Queen Anne.

While the principal wood was mahogany, much inlay of whole panels and banding was made with satinwood, fancy-grain maple or crotch-grain mahogany. Glazed doors appeared on many secretaries and cupboards. Brass door handles and oval keyhole escutcheons were present. The handles have bail drops and plates in die-stamped relief.

George Hepplewhite introduced breakfront china cabinets, breakfront secretaries, two- and three-part dining tables, half-round card tables, and sewing tables.

Sheraton (1800-1820)

Characteristics of Sheraton furniture are a predominance of straight lines, the prevailing use of slender turned and reeded legs, and delicate carving in low relief. Although it has the general appearance of lightness, Sheraton is not as delicate as Hepplewhite. Mahogany wood continued in vogue, contrasted by fancy-grain maple veneer and satinwood. The characteristic "Sheraton pull" was an oblong, stamped brass plate and bail handle, although some rosette brass knobs and lion's heads with pendant rings were also used.

Urn-shaped splats characterized earlier Sheraton chairs, while later Sheraton "French Directoire" chairs had a lyre motif and either carved or brass paw feet. The chairs had rectangular backs with a minimum of carved decoration and had stretchers. Tables were designed with lyre-shaped pedestals.

Furniture experts often lump Sheraton and Hepplewhite together and label their work "Federal" because the two styles are usually indistiguishable for the average collector. Remember, though, that their chair-back shapes, legs and sideboard configurations differed. Thus, the Sheraton sideboard is widest at its ends and the Hepplewhite widest at its center. I suppose what increases this identification problem is that American cabinetmakers copied the English designs and were not always faithful to them. One such cabinetmaker was Duncan Phyfe.

Duncan Phyfe

Phyfe was a successful cabinetmaker in New York between about 1795 and 1847. And while he was not the creative designer of any particular style, his work being influenced by his predecessors in England, he was the connecting link between Early American and American Empire furniture. His pieces, made exclusively in mahogany, were clearly attributable to his firm. Stylewise, his pieces bore a strong resemblance to Sheraton, and decorations (chiefly the acanthus), were widely used.

Today the average collector is unlikely to run across original Queen Annes, Chippendales, Hepplewhites, Phyfes or Sheratons. If there are any available for sale, they are bought at auctions or from very exclusive dealers. What one is more likely to find are very good, and perhaps very old, reproductions.

Country and Primitive furniture

Furniture made for the average home, farm home and the poor during this period has been called "Country" and "Primitive," categories open to controversy because they are a type of catchall. The difference between the two, it appears, is that Country furniture was made by country cabinetmakers who were inspired by European furniture. They rethought designs and introduced into them a strong streak of individuality.

Looking at a Country chest or chest made in 1790 in Philadelphia, I note no top frieze, no small drawers, plain escutcheons and pulls, simpler finials, less carving and detail, and a plainer wood grain which could be maple instead of the high-style cherry. In contrast, Primitive did not emulate high style or Country. Typically, this style combines many styles into one, reflecting the eclectic and inventive nature of the cabinetmaker and his concern for cost-cutting.

Primitive includes Early Ohio and Early Pennsylvania, rather nebulous classifications. Since Primitive pieces are all handmade, at times rather roughly, one can note the hand-planing of panelled door and drawer bottoms as well as the dovetails and mortise joints. Finishes were painted and natural. Painted surfaces were often false-grained; painting or false-graining such a piece cannot aesthetically survive refinishing. If the Primitive pieces had a natural finish, it was wax or shellac.

Victorian Furniture

The furniture style during Queen Victoria's reign lasted about one hundred years. It was a period characterized by great change both socially and technologically, and a time of considerable creativeness. This is obvious from the ten

This nineteenth-century reproduction of a Shaker rocker is of maple construction. It has been refinished and now has a seat that is of wide cane, rather than the traditional rushing seat.

distinctive furniture styles recognized as Victorian. Authorities divide the period of Victorian furniture into three parts: early, high and late. The periods and their respective styles are listed below; actually they are not so neatly arranged, as there were both prototypes, overlapping, reach-backs and subtypes.

Early Victorian:	American Empire	1820-1840
	Early Victorian	1840-1866
	Gothic	1840-1870
High Victorian:	Spool-Turned	1850-1880
	Cottage	1845-1890
	Renaissance	1855-1875
	Louis XV	1845-1875
Late Victorian:	Louis XVI	1865-1875
	Eastlake	1870-1890
	Golden Oak	1895-1910
	Mission Oak	1900-1920
	Art Nouveau	1895-1915

What all these Victorian period styles have in common is that they tend to be heavy, even massive. Ornamentation ran from the plain (at times) Gothic and early Eastlake to the baroque Belter and the rococo Renaissance. Wood species delineate the periods. Early Victorian and Empire featured mahogany; Gothic, Renaissance and Louis XVI pieces, walnut; and Eastlake, Golden Oak and Mission Oak, oak. Pine was the principal material of Cottage and Spool-Turned.

Early Victorian

Early Victorian furniture consisted of Empire, a separate category labelled Early Victorian and Gothic. All of it represented a considerable departure from the prior Federal period.

AMERICAN EMPIRE (1820-1840). Whenever I think of this style I see mahogany veneer, four-drawer chests with an ogee-moulded, single-cyma curved top drawer, and a frieze that's supported by heavy cyma-curved pilasters about 3 in. (7.6 cm) wide, resting on front feet as convex scrolls. Such a chest is commonly available for sale and at a relatively low price.

Empire is a continuation of late Sheraton. Its main characteristics are bulk, pillars, columns and pilasters, lavish application of crotch-grain mahogany veneer and use of ogee moulding. It was the last vestige of the pillar-and-scroll style. Scrolls were cheaply produced because of the invention of the bandsaw.

Empire ushered in the famous Boston rocker and the Hitchcock chair. The two principal restoration difficulties I have found with this style are the blistering and missing veneer, particularly from drawer fronts, and covering up the look that stripping off the old finish gives a piece.

EARLY VICTORIAN (1840-1866). In contrast to Empire, this style brought in the marble-topped table and case, substituted walnut and rosewood for mahogany, and introduced a baroqueness not present in Empire. In design, we note the return of the cabriole leg, terminating in a rudimentary foot; combining French ornateness and Gothic simplicity, this design leaned toward the ostentatious.

Refinished natural, this Primitive cupboard (c. 1830) is of a two-piece, solid 1-in. (2.5-cm)-thick cherry-wood construction. The drawer bottoms and inside door panels are hand-planed; the dovetails are hand-cut. This cupboard, small in size for the Primitive period, has glass that is held in place on the inside with putty.

Of solid pine construction, this slop chest (1840) is made of only six pieces of 1-in. (2.5-cm)-thick wood. The dovetails are hand-cut, and casters have been added to permit movement. The chest has since been refinished with oil stain and polyurethane and presently serves as a cocktail table.

Refinished natural, this Early Victorian Country chest (1850) is made of cherry wood. The pulls are of a Victorian style, but the chest is considered to be a Country piece because it has a design that is much too plain for a Victorian chest. The drawer bottoms are hand-planed, and the dovetails are hand-cut.

Characteristic of the top-of-the-line Early Victorian furniture is the Belter, sometimes called the baroque Belter. His pieces were made of six to eight layers of thin rosewood and had ornate designs cut clear through with a bandsaw.

The remaining pieces of this period, most of which are identifiable as Belter, are undulating curves, Gothic simplicity and realistic carvings of leaves, flowers and fruits done in high relief. A newcomer was the extension table with removable leaves, the ottoman and the modern bedstead.

GOTHIC (1840-1870). This style coincided with the popularity of Gothic revival architecture, and thus many of the best examples of Gothic furniture were designed (by architects such as Andrew Jackson Downing) to conform to their structural designs. This was particularly true with built-in bookcases and sideboards.

Gothic was both ornate and plain. The ornate consisted of superimposing classical forms such as scrolls and pillars on the typically tall, rectangular Gothic form. At times fanciful medieval Gothic motifs were designed into a particular piece. The plain Gothic included little of this, being characterized by pointed arched panels for glazed- or wood-panelled cabinet doors and drawer fronts, chair backs and pilasters.

Walnut has by this time become dark, almost black—a color achieved by applying an acid wash to the wood. That and rosewood continued to be popular, although some mahogany appeared on occasional tables. Spool turnings were common on legs, trestle supports, bedposts, chair-back uprights and spindles.

Newly introduced furniture pieces were the secretary with folded-over flaps, sidechairs and matching bedroom suites. Tables and sofas, however, are not found in this style.

High Victorian

While some of the styles introduced in the previous period continued to be produced (Gothic in particular), this segment of Victoriana witnessed some new designs. They are Spool-Turned, Cottage, Renaissance and Louis XV.

SPOOL-TURNED (1850-1880). Getting its name from spool turnings for legs, trestle supports, bedposts, uprights and spindles, this style has the distinction of being the first truly mass-produced furniture. Although it may have made its appearance as early as 1815, Spool-Turned certainly paved the path for the Eastlake style.

Since various makers of spool furniture used almost any wood that was available, the value of any particular piece is a factor of its raw material. Mahogany was the standard for top-of-the-line pieces, notably small occasional tables. One will also find some made from black walnut, maple and birch. Pine, however, was much more common.

This Gothic Victorian wardrobe (1860) is identifiable as "Gothic" from its arched door panels. It is constructed of walnut and is made of seven assemblies held together with large pegs and holes. It has been refinished with natural varnish and shellac.

All woods were stained to resemble mahogany, no matter what their species, and here rests a major restoration problem: trying to get all of the mahogany stain out of the spool turnings. The end grain of the wood is exposed on both sides of each bulb, and this porous surface soaks in the stain more than the outside of the bulb does. My experience restoring spool beds is that I live with the mahogany color and brush on a color-correcting stain after the stripping process.

Worse than the old mahogany stain is the spool-turned piece some handyman has painted. Long soaking with stripper before any attempt at finish removal and careful use of a wire brush is most effective. But it does take time!

Spool-turned beds are a commonly encountered restoration piece. In all, there are three typical variations. One has both head and footboard with spool-turned posts, two cross rails and slender spool-turned spindles. The second differs in that it features quarter-round turned segments that join the top rail and the post. The third style variation has a plain one-piece headboard with the upper edge surmounted with spool-turned cresting; the footboard has a smaller plain board similarly surmounted and has spindles below it to a cross rail below.

COTTAGE (1845-1890). Cottage furniture is a loose classification of pieces made just before the American Civil War and for 30 years afterward that don't fit in any other category. They are made of pine, resemble Early American in line, and were inexpensive, painted, mass-produced and mass-marketed (mostly by mail order).

Although Early Cottage was based on Empire designs, Late Cottage was simpler. It may well be that your "Early American" piece is Cottage with its original paint removed.

Cottage spool may even resemble early Spool-Turned. Remember though, that Spool-Turned often used native hardwoods and was invariably stained mahogany. There are generally two distinguishing differences between Cottage and Early American: cabinet hinges and drawer dovetails. Earlier pieces had hand-cut dovetails, and hand-forged, long, thin or butterfly hinges.

Common Cottage pieces are painted pine washstands, dry sinks, Shaker chests of drawers and Renaissance-style commodes.

LOUIS XV (1845-1875). Both the ornateness and the era of its popularity places this style in the High Victorian period. Characteristically curvilinear in marked contrast to the perpendicular line of Renaissance, Louis XV is perhaps best illustrated in upholstered sofas, especially the well-known medallion sofa. This style also introduced upholstered gentlemen's armchairs and upholstered ladies' chairs, all of which were often combined to form the first parlour suite. In drawing rooms of the period, several side chairs were added; sofas, couches or love seats would be in pairs, and perhaps matching étagères would also be present.

Extensive use was made of dark walnut and some native hardwoods as well. Dowel construction was now replacing the tenon-and-mortise joint of preceding periods. Finger-moulded carvings was prominent on these pieces.

RENAISSANCE (1855-1875). This was the furniture of Abraham Lincoln's time, derived in part from the Empire period, elaborate as in early Victorian, often tall as Gothic, yet innovative in the use of applied mouldings. A function of Renaissance architecture, this furniture style also had tall arched pediments, large carved cartouches (carved or inlaid unrolled scrolls or oval tablets) and burl-veneer panels.

The principal wood was walnut that was made dark, although cheaper furniture grades used pine that was stained in order to imitate mahogany or rosewood. Swirling lines of black ink were applied to imitate the more expensive grains and are very difficult to remove. Characteristic of this style are wooden drawer pulls, with carved motifs of fruit, leaves and scrolls. Keyhole rosettes were wooden.

Significant pieces of this period are the secretaries and desks for libraries and offices. In addition, there were the circular, marble-topped parlor tables, the rectangular library tables with baize-panelled top and the trestle sewing table. Other typical Renaissance pieces are chests of four drawers with carved walnut handles, bureaus with handkerchief drawers and tall tilt mirrors, and tall, elaborate bed headboards.

Late Victorian

The Victorian period ended on a lighter note, both in terms of furniture color and in terms of furniture mass. Principal styles were Louis XVI, Eastlake, Golden Oak, Art Nouveau and Mission Oak. As the latter style is such a departure from Victoriana, one could easily challenge its inclusion. I guess the reason why I do is that those influential in its design certainly had their roots in the Victorian era.

LOUIS XVI (1865-1875). Less popular than Louis XV, this style lasted only ten years. In contrast to the curved outline and cabriole legs of Louis XV, the later design, which used primarily walnut, featured slender, tapered legs. Arms were open or rudimentary, carvings were replaced with burl panels, and chair legs were braced with turned H-shaped stretchers. Plainer than Louis XV, Louis XVI was both a reaction to the ornateness of its predecessors and served as an introduction to the rather plain Eastlake design.

EASTLAKE (1870-1890). Victoriana ended with two very popular furniture styles manufactured in relatively large quantities. They are Eastlake, named for architect Charles Eastlake, and Golden Oak. Eastlake was made with black walnut but ash, oak, chestnut, cherry and maple were later used as well.

The characteristic line is straight and the shape rectilinear; decor was usually vertical, and horizontal incised lines accentuated the overall line of the piece. Drawer fronts had horizontal lines, and chest fronts vertical ones. Machines cut shallow geometric designs. Burl veneer panels were common. Legs are square or tapered, but not curved. As such, Eastlake was the forerunner of Mission. Although this style began as an uncluttered and functional one, it acquired ornateness as the period progressed.

Much Eastlake furniture was evidently cheaply made. Chest and door panels and drawer bottoms are much thinner than typically Victorian pieces. Dovetails were circular in many Eastlake pieces, providing a quick means of identification. Pulls were pendant rings or bails with shaped plates and escutcheons. China casters continued in use from early Victorian times.

Perhaps the principal furniture innovation of this era is the platform rocker, although the rocker was available in Renaissance times. Its popularity during this period resembled the popularity of the recliner today. Other than the platform rocker, Eastlake continued to make the pieces of the past, although upholstered furniture was not as common as all-wood pieces. Eastlake was a sort of a reform style. Its straight lines, lighter color and relative plainness appear to have been a reaction to ornate Victorian styles.

GOLDEN OAK (1895-1910). The lighter shades introduced by Eastlake were retained by the Golden Oak style, but the straight lines were not. Golden Oak has a kind of Early American look to it at times in that it is often curvilinear, featuring turnings, bowed-front chests, curved-back rockers, round oak tables, rolltop desks and pressed-back chairs. The style ranges from the plain of Eastlake to a Renaissance Victorian, having carved or applied decor, trim, mouldings or pressings.

Golden Oak was often "golden ash"; that is, the cheaper and easier to work ash was substituted for oak, or combined with oak in the same piece. The natural lightness of the woods was enhanced in the factory. Today, refinishers generally let the natural warm color of oak and ash shine through. The pieces are finished "natural"; many of the Golden Oak pieces were originally somewhat darker.

Tops are made of several boards glued together, and backboards are very thin sheets of a softwood. Drawers often have no dovetailing and are assembled with routed cuts and glue and nails. Pressed-back chairs have both their designs and their curves created by steam and by pressure. Different woods were often used in the same piece. Though furniture makers were sophisticated enough to match the colors of the woods perfectly, modern restorers are not nearly so clever. Hence "natural" finish may expose the color differences of the wood species. That is why I will often use a stain on such pieces; it gives a color evenness that natural finish often does not.

Made of turned legs and solid oak top and shelf, this Golden Oak plant table has been refinished with oil and polyurethane.

MISSION OAK (1900-1920). Mission got its name from the California missions. This design was part of the Arts and Crafts Movement promulgated by Gustav Stickley, which also included his bungalow architectural style. Stickley's name is actually on some Mission furniture. Other important designers included Frank Lloyd Wright, initiator of the Prairie School of Architecture, and Greene and Greene, brothers who revolutionized California architecture.

Though not nearly so important as Golden Oak, Mission *is* a significant design. Characteristically linear and vertical, it is certainly masculine and in some respects a modern Gothic. The principal wood used is oak and the typical color a very dark brown. This color was achieved in some instances by fuming, but I believe more typically by applying a very dark brown stain, or varnish-stain. The Mission furniture was often uncomfortable to use and without superfluous lines.

Mission furniture, in addition to being assembled in the traditional vein, uses the unconcealed round-head wood screw, which is functional and decorative.

Not a traditional antique, and predicted by some authorities never to be found in an antique shop (they were wrong), Mission desks, chairs, dining suites and case goods have become the new antiques, particularly in the Midwest and on the West Coast. Mission's popularity among collectors has much to do with its simple design (and therefore simple restoration), its ability to fit the eclectic furnishing of today, and its generally lower price.

ART NOUVEAU (1895-1915). This is primarily a European design, and World War One was probably the cause of its demise.

The characteristic decor of Art Nouveau is derived from nature, be it flowers, leaves, vines or trees. It is always representational or abstract, however, and has a great deal of inlaying, marquetry and moulding. Fine woods, such as rosewood, were often used because much of this furniture probably was custom-made. More typically, the material was plain, unvarnished oak. The graceful curves of this style readily lent itself to the use of metal, its first important introduction as a furniture material.

The Twentieth Century

Art Deco (1920-1935)

In its time, Art Deco was the modern art. In furniture, it was characterized by simplicity of design, often curvilinear line, a built-in look, light woods and veneers and painted surfaces. There was a new functionality which called for little decor, ornamentation and carving; decorative woods, metal and glass were extensively used. Some of the decorative woods were laurel, Macassar ebony, Nigerian walnut, Bombay rosewood, Canadian birch, Australian silky oak and Indian padauk.

The Mission Oak display cabinet shown here is made of solid oak, and the small "panes" of glass are actually three large pieces of glass that have mullions (strips of wood) placed over them. Refinishing was done with oil stain and polyurethane.

The pressed-back construction of this early twentieth-century chair entailed putting a design into the chair back with steam and pressure, machine-embossing, or a combination of these processes. This cherry-wood chair was made in New England and has a sheet-caned bottom.

The painted designs were usually geometric, in contrast to the flora and fauna of Art Nouveau. Art Deco was decidedly more cheery and brighter than anything in the past. It ushered in a decor of light color, often brilliancy, from rugs to walls to window treatment. Though it was often light in mass, at times Art Deco was oppressively heavy. Frank Lloyd Wright, for example, designed some furniture made of light-colored plywood as one would design solid concrete pieces, resulting in visual heaviness.

Art Deco is definitely collectible; however, any painted pieces you may acquire will have to remain painted to hold their value for the future. And any metal, leather or specially glazed pieces will require special treatment if they are in need of repair. It has been my experience that you will not find a lot of Art Deco around. It was an unpopular design at a time when the public was not buying too much furniture anyway due to World Wars One and Two, and the Depression.

William and Mary Revival (1920–1935)

This type of furniture, whose name I have coined, was in a sense Depression furniture. Like its seventeenth-century originator, this furniture was all legs. Cabinets, buffets, dining tables and side chairs all have rather long, inverted cup legs, carved bun feet, and serpentine stretchers that are frequently crossed, with finials at intersections. There is a feeling of openness and lightness in such pieces, but the forest of legs is surely present. The principal woods were walnut and oak; cheaper pieces used panels of poplar or birch-stained walnut.

The backs of chairs were often high; some carved and caned. Some chair legs also had a pear-shaped bulb. This style is also currently collectible, though this furniture is not considered to be antique. It is available in complete dining suites and bedroom suites.

Contemporary

This being a book on antiques, I will comment only on antique reproduction pieces now available, the European antiques, and antiques of the future.

It would appear that the scope of reproduction furniture is increasing. Formerly only "Colonial" furniture was available in stores. Now one sees more and more Victorian pieces. While most of the items I have seen are not good copies, a few are very good. You may want to complete your decor with some of them. For example, a customer for whom I restored a lovely Victorian round pedestal dining table made of mahogany was unable to get antique chairs for it. So she bought reproduction chairs that were unfinished and finished them to match her table. Everything goes together beautifully.

The William and Mary Revival desk shown at left is a good example of the high, leggy pieces made in the late 1920s and early Thirties. Refinished natural, it has a walnut veneer except for its solid members.

Many European antiques are being sold in the United States, though it is my guess that they are not terribly old; they probably came out of European hotels, resorts and convents.

Looking at the really valuable antique pieces of today, one is struck with the fact that most of them were quite dear even in their day. Belter, for example, was very expensive in early Victorian times. So if you insist on saving contemporary pieces, save an original Eames chair, an unusual, unique, one-of-a-kind Herman Miller or something a museum or furniture authority rates highly. On items such as those you may realize a profit in your lifetime.

Glossary

acanthus ornamentation	a type of ornamentation that represents the leaves of the acanthus, a prickly herb
bail drops	the movable part of a drawer pull
baize	a coarse woollen or cotton fabric
bevel	the angular cut of door panels, drawer bottoms, etc.
birdseye	having circular or elliptical figures that resemble birds' eyes
brad	a small nail
bleeding	the amalgamation or muddying-up of furniture stain
burls	roundish outgrowths on a tree
cabriole legs	curved legs of furniture that have out-curved knees and incurved ankles
cambric	a thin, black material
case goods	furniture that has interior storage space
caul	a small piece of wood used with metal clamps to protect furniture wood from being crushed by the clamp
close-grained	refers to wood that has narrow annual rings
crossbar	the horizontal part of a chair back
crotch grain	part at which a tree splits or branches out
cyma	the "C" curve on furniture legs, feet of pedestal tables and case front columns of the Empire period

dovetail	method of joining drawer fronts to sides, chest fronts to sides. The older the piece of furniture, the fewer the dovetails
escutcheon	an ornamental or protective shield of metal
fiddleback	a fine, wavy wood grain
figure	refers to wood grain, i.e., "figured" grain
finials	crowning ornamental detail
frieze	part of a cabinet that is just below the top moulding. It is usually straight and vertical and may or may not have a design
gimp	decorative braided material
heartwood	the wood in the center of a tree trunk or limb
lap-joined	case-back construction in which panels are glued into vertical, grooved moulding pieces
long-ray	long lines in wood grain that run perpendicular to the grain
marriage	occurs when two similar pieces of furniture are put together to make one piece
mortise joints	point at which wood pieces are fastened together, featuring a male and female piece. Used before dowel-joining and used with a tenon as a mortise-and-tenon joint
ogee-moulded	moulded with a single or double cyma curve
pad foot	a chair or table foot that looks like the paw of an animal

pilastre	half-column decoration on case goods
plinth	the foot or base of a column
quarter-sawing	sawing wood so that the rings form an angle of 45–90 degrees with the wide surface of the piece
rift cut	lumber-mill cut of a log that is made to produce long wood rays
rococo	excessive carving or applied moulding for decorative purposes
roey	curly
sapwood	pale-colored wood near the outside of a log
satinwood	a lustrous, yellow-brownish wood in the mahogany family
skirt	part of a table that is just below the tabletop
splat	part of a chair back that is flat board. It can be used with or without spindles.
spline	cane material which holds sheet cane in place
straight-grained	fibres that run parallel to the length of the tree
tack cloth	cheesecloth that has been impregnated with a substance to facilitate removal of dust, lint, sand, etc., from a furniture surface
tenon	a cut or fit for insertion into a mortise. Used with mortise, as in mortise-and-tenon joint
turned chair	chair legs, spindles, etc., that are turned on a lathe

Index